Drawing Nature

Mastering simple projects (Practical guide)

Brenda Clark

Copyright©2018 Brenda Clark
All Rights Reserved

Copyright © 2018 by Brenda Clark

All rights reserved. No part of this publication may be reproduced, distributed, or transmitted in any form or by any means, including photocopying, recording, or other electronic or mechanical methods, without the prior written permission of the author, except in the case of brief quotations embodied in critical reviews and certain other noncommercial uses permitted by copyright law.

Table of Contents

Introduction	**6**
Materials for drawing	**8**
How to Start Draw	**10**
Techniques base	**15**
Geometrical figures	**19**
Picture 1. 3D Cube	19
Picture 2. 3D Pyramid	21
Picture 3. Cylindrical rectangle	23
Picture 4. Lying cylinder	25
Picture 5. Sphere	27
Flowers	**29**
Picture 6. Stalks	29
Picture 7. Weeping Petals	32
Picture 8. Pointed Leaves	36
Picture 9. Small Flowers	39
Picture 10. Pretty Petals	43
Picture 11. Simple Flower	47
Picture 12. Fanning Leaf	49
Picture 13. Rose and Leaves	54
Picture 14. Bouquet	57
Trees	**60**
Picture 15. Basic Tree	60
Picture 16. Leafy Tree	64
Picture 17. Tall Palm	68
Picture 18. Thin Branched Tree	71
Picture 19. Basic Tree Part 2	74
Animals	**79**
Picture 20. Dragonfly	79
Picture 21. Snail	83
Picture 22. Parrot	86
Picture 23. Penguin	90

Picture 24. Crawfish	95
Picture 25. Wallaby	99
Picture 26. Fish	103
Picture 27. Octopus	106
Picture 28. Dog	109
Picture 29. Lion and Cub	113
Picture 30. Fox	117
Picture 31. Antelope	120
Picture 32. Vulture	123
Picture 33. Stegosaurus	126
Landscapes	**128**
Picture 34. City Streets	128
Picture 35. Mountain Ridge	134
Picture 36. Valley Road	138
Picture 37. Ruin Structure	142
Conclusion	**147**

Disclaimer

While all attempts have been made to verify the information provided in this book, the author does assume any responsibility for errors, omissions, or contrary interpretations of the subject matter contained within. The information provided in this book is for educational and entertainment purposes only. The reader is responsible for his or her own actions and the author does not accept any responsibilities for any liabilities or damages, real or perceived, resulting from the use of this information.

The trademarks that are used are without any consent, and the publication of the trademark is without permission or backing by the trademark owner. All trademarks and brands within this book are for clarifying purposes only and are the owned by the owners themselves, not affiliated with this document.

Introduction

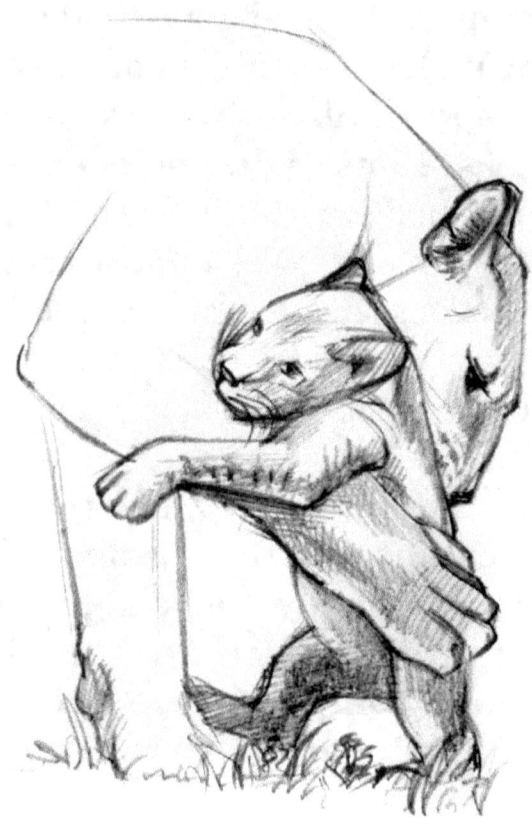

Welcome to the Beginners Guide to Drawing Nature! In this book you will learn about how to draw elements and aspects of nature. You will learn about the techniques and the skills required drawing very carefully crafted images of nature. What kinds of images of nature you might be asking? Well, we will start out with animals and insects of various kinds and types. There are around 14 different creatures to draw. Then we will move on to a variety of flowers and foliage, a total of 14 images in that category as well. Then to cap it off we will illustrate 4 different engaging backgrounds that really capitalize on nature's beauty as a whole.

Each one of these images will have several steps included in it to show you how you get from the very inception and conception of the idea and then you will be shown how to build up from it and turn it into the finished product. Each of these will vary in difficulty and ultimately culminate in you learning the skills required to tackle images like these on your own and know how to start and what materials you will need. More than you will learn how to carry the project through to completion step by step. This book is a great assistant to any artist of any skill level looking to either branch out or fine tune their skill set and level into something more nature based and oriented. It doesn't matter what you already know, or if you have more experience, you will find valuable information in these pages. Without dragging this introduction on for too long let's move on and get into the materials that you will need for this project!

Materials for drawing

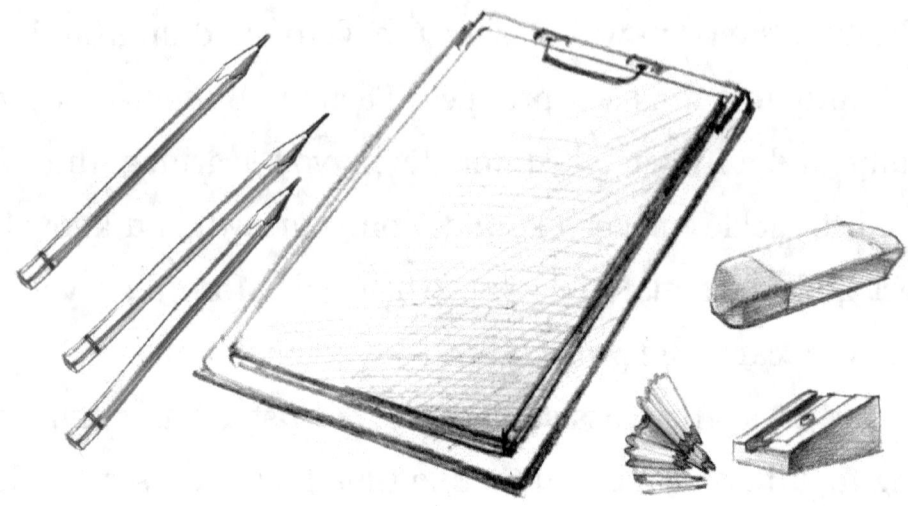

Above you will see an image that is most likely fairly self explanatory. However I wouldn't be doing my job of instructing and guiding you if I didn't get into it and explain what you're looking at. The materials laid out in the image are the things you will need to embark on the images in this book and to successfully craft and design your own images of nature. These are important because each one of these offers different opportunities to improve and proceed with your art.

The pencil is fairly obvious, but having multiple is important as well. For instance if one of the pencils keeps breaking its lead, you might need another one. Perhaps one of the pencils gets dull quickly then instead of spending forever sharpening you can just swap it with another one if you're in the groove of drawing.

The pencil sharpener is also pretty obvious, however I would just like to say that you do need one, and you should try to find one that looks like the one in the image, with this style of sharpener you get to see how its sharpening your pencil and can tell if it is cutting the lead or if its sharp enough.

An eraser is also fairly clear, but the reason why you can't just use the ones on the back of your pencil is because these other ones offer a more precise method of erasing and won't smudge your image.

The pencil shavings you see in the image are purely an example of artistry and is indicative of the kind of drawing you'll learn in this book.

Last item depicted that you need is a clipboard. The reason why we suggest a clipboard is because it's something that you can turn and angle easily without losing control of your page or perhaps even creasing it or bending it. It offers more control and enables you to be more precise.

An item that isn't pictured but that you might want would be that of a straight edge ruler, it can help with the lines that are trickier and might need a solid edge, so it would be a good idea to have one on hand.

How to Start Draw

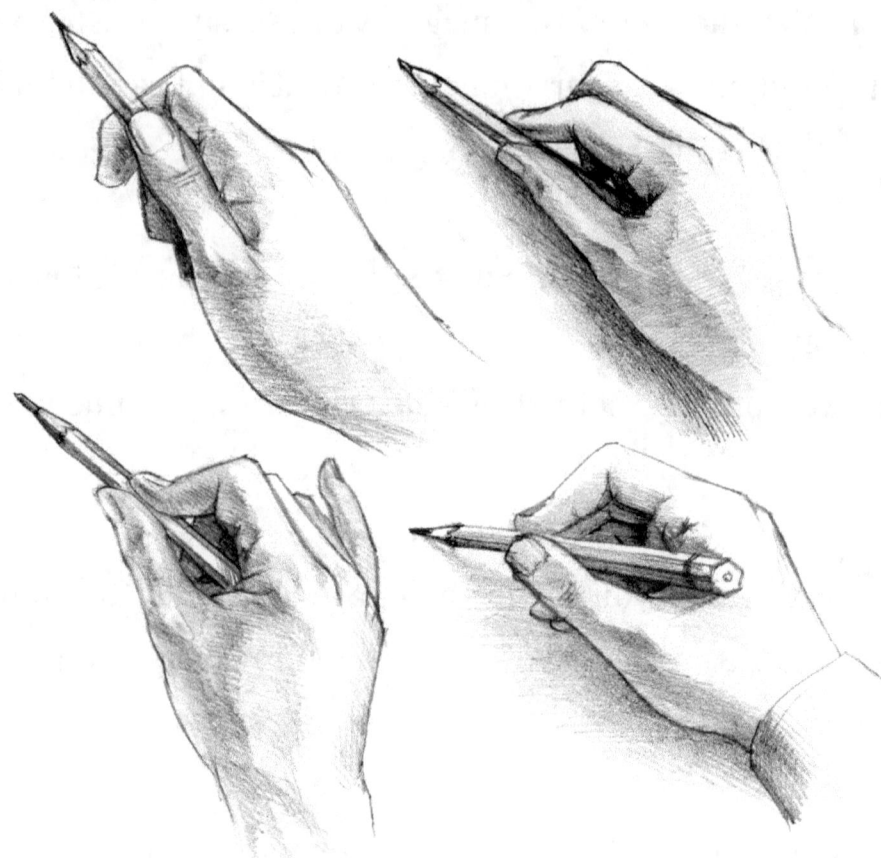

Now that you have your materials gathered you will probably want to just jump right in and start your drawings. However for the sake of getting the most you can out of this book there are two more stops before you dive right in. This section, titled 'How to start' is going to be a brief and concise but incredibly important section about exactly that concept. How do you start your drawing? It isn't enough to just pick up a pencil and then put it to paper and hope all goes well. There is some knowledge required and there is a certain level of skill that is expected of you as well. For instance, how do you hold the pencil? As well as that, do you know your composition of the image?

That last part is fairly easy in this book because we lay out the composition for you in the steps provided with each image you will be working on. Which is one less thing for you to worry about but still something you should know about? In this section you are going to learn about some special terminologies associated with drawing as well as the basic way of holding your pencil.

Perception - This may be one of the most important aspects of drawing, because it is entirely how you see the image and then translate that to the paper. Are you looking at your subject head on, are you drawing it from the side, is there lighting.

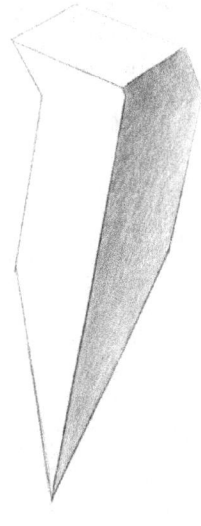

Composition - This is essentially the set up of the image, how it all comes to together. It is a way of showcasing what it is that you are expressing and highlights the areas of great importance in the image.

Proportion - Something that changes based on the age and structure of your subject. For instance if you were to draw a baby animal and then draw the same animal once its aged, the proportions would change and this should be reflected in the drawing.

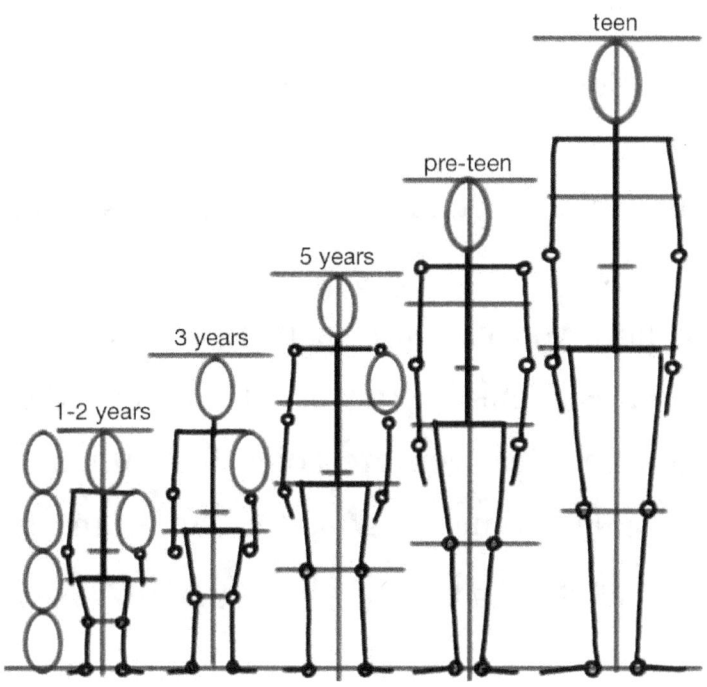

Tone - Based almost entirely on the usage of light and shadows within the drawing itself. This is important, because tone can essentially pave the way for your composition and utilizes your perception of the subject carefully. You need to truly pay attention to where your light source is and know of the subject's highlights or shadows.

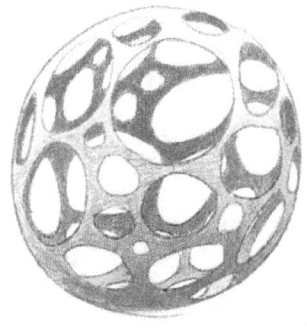

These 4 are some of the most important variables in a beginners drawing education. Without these it becomes increasingly difficult to be able to layout or proceed with a drawing because you don't have some of the most useful elements at play.

To the right here you can see an image of how to handle the pencil for your sketching/drawing. These are the best ways depending on the effect you are going for with the pencil. For instance the top left would be good for harder and thicker lines. Then the top right is excellent for shading or blending.

The bottom left is an excellent one to use for thinner and softer lines, and then the bottom right is just the basic and most simple way of holding a pencil for drawing.

With this information in this section, you are just about ready to get started on these drawings. Just one more section to go and you can begin!

Techniques base

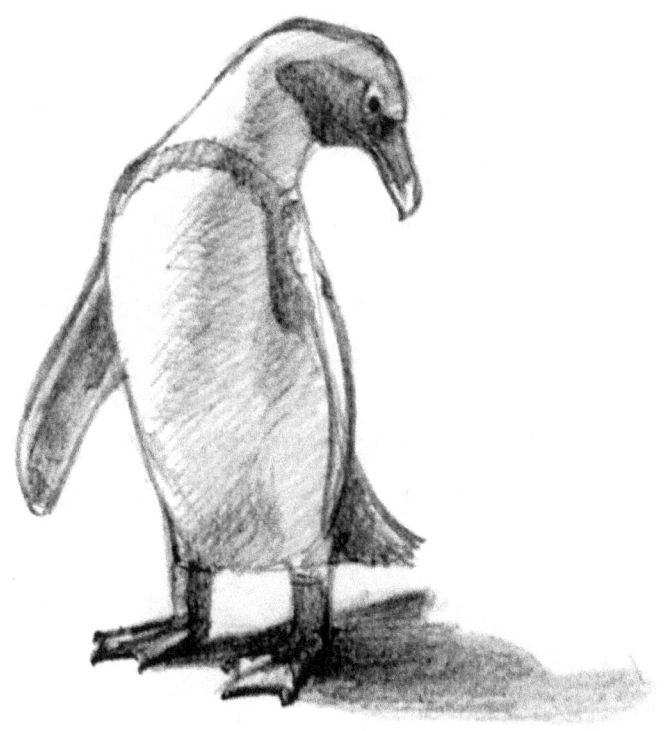

You are now one step closer to being able to dive into the wonderful exercises contained in this work book! In the final chapter before you actually get to do some practice drawings I want to go over several of the techniques you will be utilizing in this workbook. There is a lot more to drawing and sketching than just putting pencil to paper and making lines and such. There is so much in fact that you would need multiple books to learn everything! However this book contains everything you need to start out and successfully sketch the drawings contained within these pages and build up your portfolio and knowledge base of art quite a lot. Without any more to say let's get into some of the techniques you will be getting involved with in these pages.

Shading - Probably one of the most important things you'll learn in these pages is how to shade properly. Shading has everything to do with the lighting in the drawing and is something you should always plan and plot out before you even begin trying to do it. You need to take into account the light source, reflective surfaces such as water or glass, and so many things. The best way to do it is to spend some time playing with your subjects shadow in the real world before you put it down on paper.

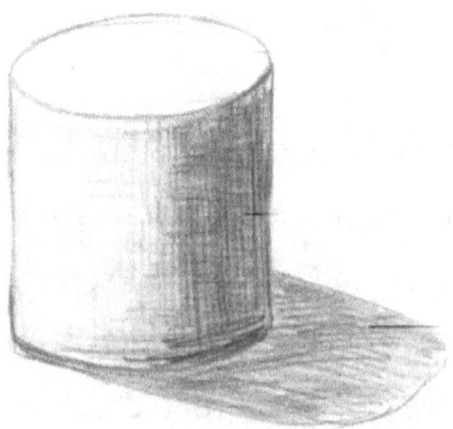

Lining - Mentioned very briefly in the last chapter, the lining is a crucial aspect and portion of the drawing. Which is why you need to know what type of lining you will be doing? You can have heavy weighted lines, or soft and light lines. You can have a mixture of the two as well. For instance something that is fluffy like a tail you might use soft lining for, but something solid like a tree you may use heavier lines for. Something to ponder before you put the pencil onto the paper.

Drafting - One of the tricks that is often overlooked by beginning artists due to the repetitious factor is that of drafting. It can be nice to do a sketch once and then walk away, but in the frame of perfection its best to always do drafts. Complete a sketch, and then improve on it in a second sketch, then do it again for a third. You'll be able to see the areas that you need to improve on as well as the areas that you excel in. It's best to practice this as often as you can and not overlook the opportunities to grow as an artist.

Texture - Much like shading, texture is a very important aspect of all drawing/artistic ventures. It is something that is largely created out of repeating patterns localized to a specific area or concept. For instance if you have a drawing of a room and the half room is carpeted while the other half is wood. How would you differentiate the texture? There is stippling which means using many small dots very close together. It can be great for carpeting or even facial hair on a man. There is hatching which are many small straight lines grouped together. It's a great method for shading in general but you can also apply it to texturizing. Another great one is cross-hatching. It is similar to hatching but with another set of lines crossing over the initial batch. This one is especially great for fabrics or other darker shading that needs to be done.

Blending - Blending is a sort of form of shading though instead of using just the pencil you can use an eraser or a dedicated blending tool? This is a way of creating softer shades and textures that appear very smooth and relaxed. It adds a very realistic look to your images as well.

Now that you have learned the basic techniques you will be using in these drawings. It is time to move onto a practice section just before we get into the real reason why you're here. The nature drawings! So enjoy these practice images and hone those skills!

Geometrical figures

Picture 1. 3D Cube

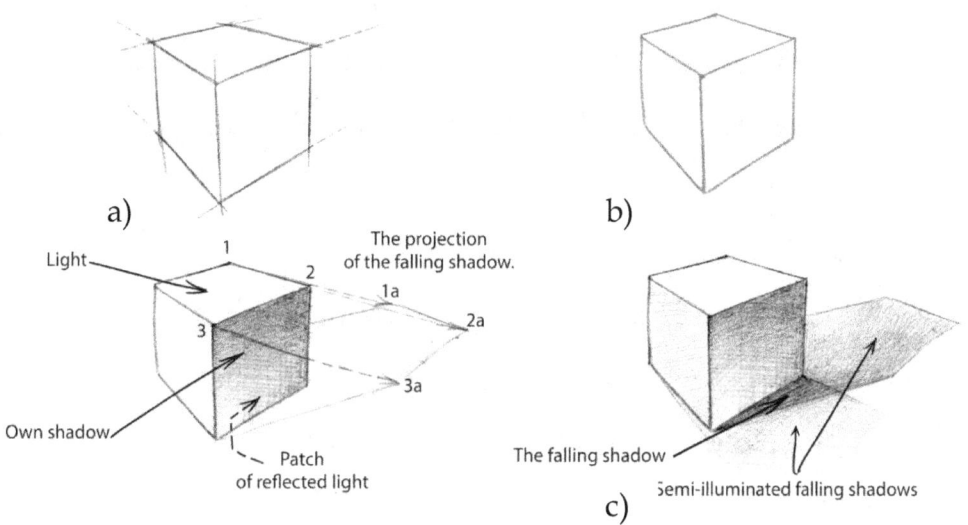

In this first practice image you can see we start fairly simple. It is a 3d cube (a). Nothing too terribly daunting yet there is definitely still skill required.

Do as is asked in the first step and draw those lines nice and sharp like to create the outline. (a)

Then in second step clean them up by erasing the excess so you are left with just the cube itself (b). It looks nice and sharp, with some soft lining at play.

The third step here is where you figure out your light source and plan out the shading (1a). As mentioned in the last chapter it is always best to plan what your shading will look like before you just jump into it and start shading things. So you can see that the standing is plotted using the corners of the cube itself to line up where the shadow would fall in the event of a light coming from the left hand side of the cube (2a/3a).

In the final step we shade in the cube as plotted in the third step. If you look closely you can see that it's a cross hatch on the cube itself and then more of just a basic hatch on the shading on the actual floor of the cube? (c)

Excellent work is on the first practice image. Once you feel comfortable with your work on this one move on to the next!

Picture 2. 3D Pyramid

This next image is another great exercise in shading. You can see already by an overview that it introduces another new concept into the mix. Start out by drawing the shape, and then move onto the next step (a).

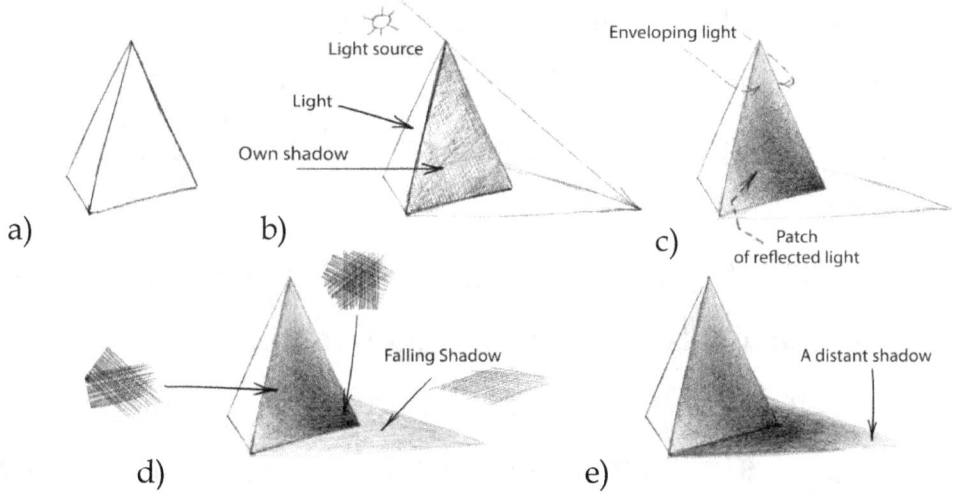

Here we add in the light source again and plot the lines that the shading will follow to create the falling shadow. As well we are now incorporating the shapes own shadow into the mix here too. Once you have those things mapped out on your drawing move onto the next step (b).

Here we start adding more density to the shading on the side of the shape as well as taking into account the reflected lights effect on the shading of the shape itself. At the top of the shape we also have something called the enveloping light (c). Which applies to narrower points that the light source hits? These are places where the light actually works its way around the edge slightly on more narrow structures or appendages.

In this next step we have a couple examples of the shading as well as we start on the falling shadow. You can see that it's calling for much thicker shading near the bottom right corner of the shape and thinner shading everywhere else. This is very realistic and creates a nice looking texture as well (d).

Finally we deal with a brand new term, "distant shadow" (e). This is when the shadow is being stretched out and naturally lightens as it's elongated. You can see this in effect in this image as the shadow stretches further away from the shape. This is where good and light blending can make the shading seem much softer and more natural.

Picture 3. Cylindrical rectangle

Now we are on to the next practice image. This is one a cylindrical rectangle. As you can see it starts out very simple as the cube (a). However the purpose of this practice sketch is to focus on the shading techniques discussed previously. So once you've drawn the main outline move on to the next step which is the purposeful shading information.

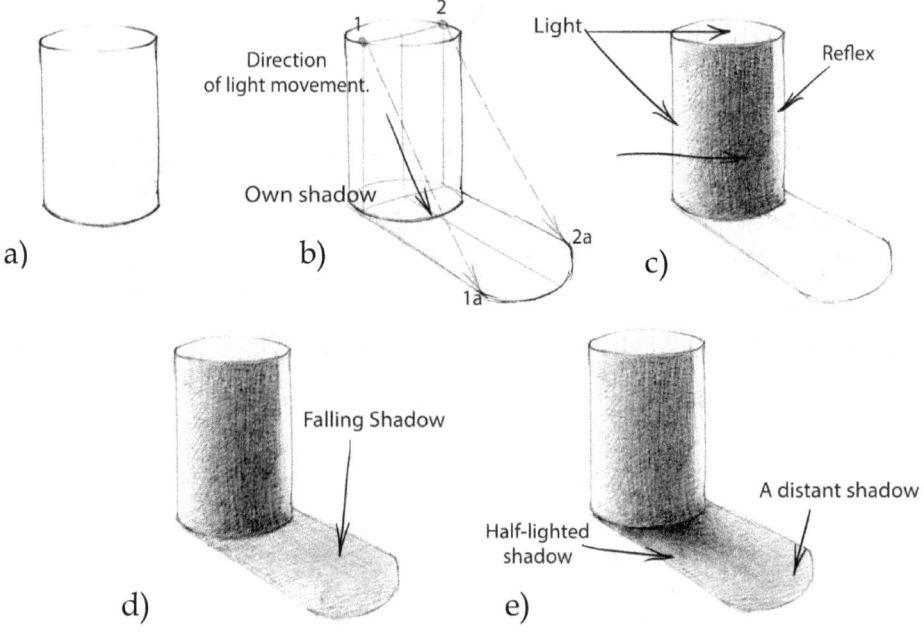

Here we plot very carefully the shading of the cylinder. You can see that there are two points that serve as the main guideline of the shape. This creates a very structured plan to be able to shade the image appropriately (b).

Then we move to step three and shade in the shape itself. You can see we use the cross hatch here as well. If you pay attention you can see that it is very thickly and densely shaded in the middle of the shape. This is where there is the least light on the image itself (c).

Next we shade the "Falling Shadow" which is the terminology for as you guessed it, where the shadow falls. This is a fairly simple shading procedure which mostly uses a light and soft hatch to start (d).

Finally, in the last step we get a little more in depth with the shading procedure. Here we take into account where the shading would be the strongest in the falling shadow. Which for future reference is usually always closest to the base of the image? (e)

Picture 4. Lying cylinder

Here we take the shape we used last, and this time takes a look at it on its side. The first step we want to take into account is the drawing of the image itself when it's on the side. You can see that the top line and bottom line is fairly simple, but it's the ends that require some attention. You can quarter the end that faces out in order to get the proportions right as shown in the first step (a).

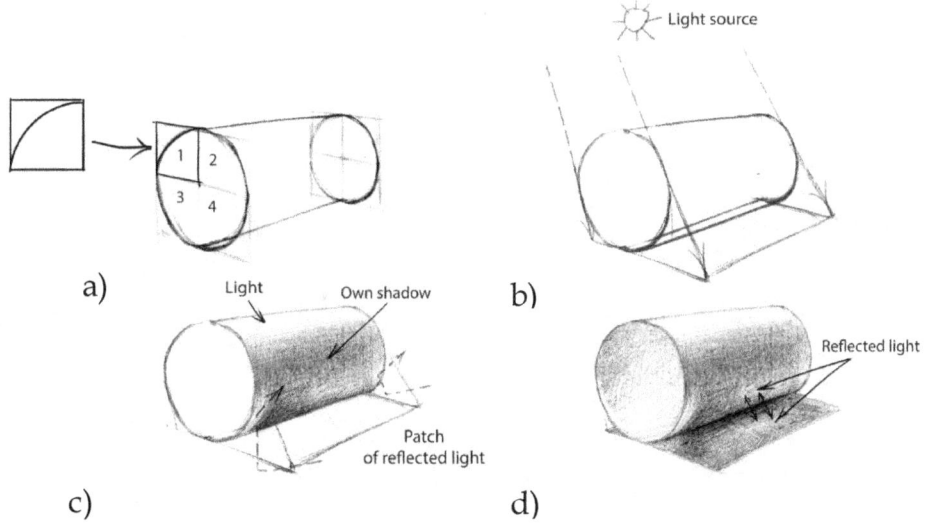

Them we actually look at where the light source would be and draw lines that coordinate exactly where the shadow would fall to (b).

Next we start our shading. Again we use a nice cross hatch on the body of the shape to get the shading started. Look closely again and see where the shading is the densest and where it's a little more blended into the light (c).

The last step is probably the most interested because we actually see the use of reflected light. Which does soften the shading in the middle of both the shape and the fallen shadow? This is something to take into account whenever doing a drawing, especially when you're doing something that is any sort of reflective material (d).

Picture 5. Sphere

This is the final practice image until you get to really sink your teeth into the Nature Drawings contained in these pages. You can see that this final image incorporates all of the skills and terms you've just learnt into one final image. Start out by drawing a circle and then use the hatch shading technique along the left side of the image (a). You can see that to begin with your just focusing on the own shadow of the shape.

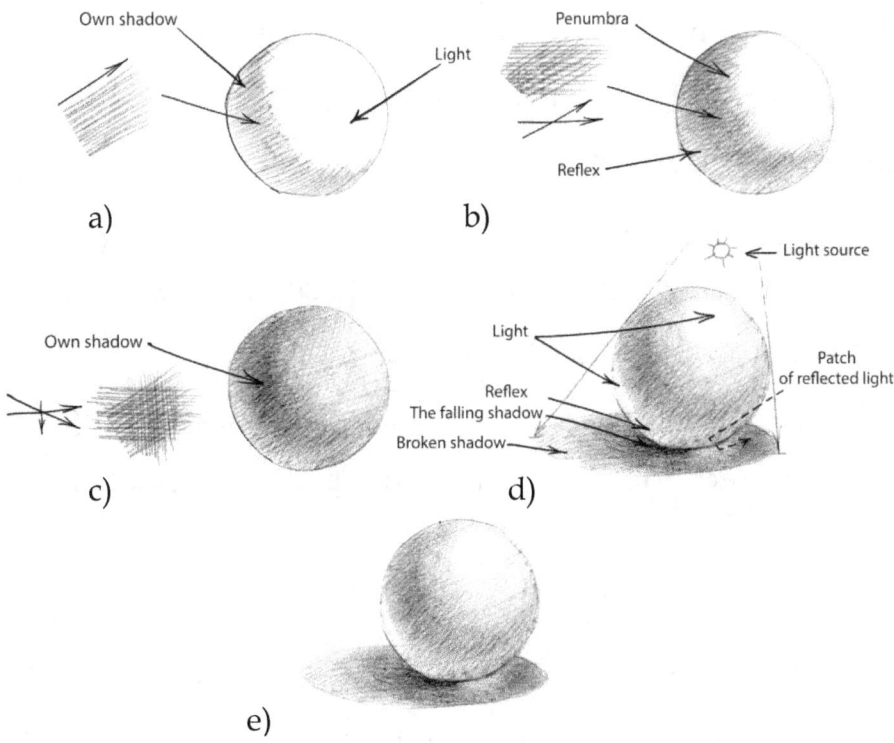

Next up we add in the more technical aspects of the shading such as the "Penumbra" which means partially shaded. As well as the

Reflex which is another way of referencing the reflected lighting from the surface the ball sits on (b).

Next set we finished the shapes own shadow by adding in some cross hatching. Make sure to keep in perspective where the lightest and densest portions of the shading reside (c).

This next step we add in the light source and the guidelines for that. You can see there is another portion of reflected light reflected by the addition of the light source. As well the falling shadow is outlined. The broken shadow refers to the space that comes in contact with extra light due to the rounded surface that the light source glides across (d).

You can see the culmination of all these shading techniques in the finished product which looks as realistic as can be with the expert shading. Here you can tell exactly where the light source stems from and don't need to wonder about any of its shading (e).

That's it for the practice drawings! Now it is time for you to get started on the first section of real nature drawings that you get to do! There are 14 in total so enjoy them while they last!

Flowers

Picture 6. Stalks

The very first entry in the flower section is this image of some thin stalks with tiny branch like leaves. This image is crazy simple and is the best way to start out this section.

You'll want to keep in mind how thin this plant is but also mind the light shading that is required on the thin stalks (a, b, c).

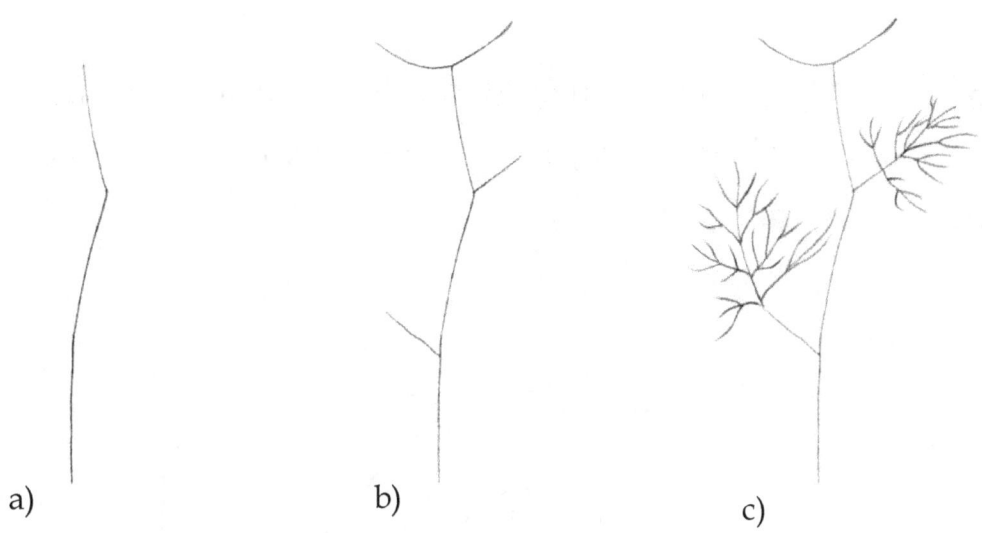

a) b) c)

Also there is some detail to consider for the very tiny flowers at the top of the plant in the final step.

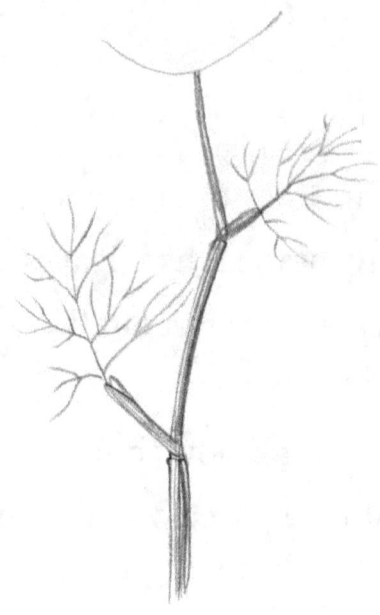

This drawing really doesn't require much instruction and should be seen as a break and a way to flex some of your expertise that you've gained from the book thus far.

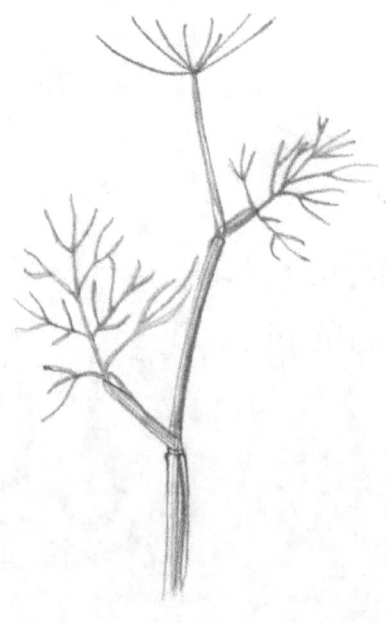

Enjoy this drawing and find a way to spice it up if you do so choose, add a background, sketch in one of the animals from the last section and make it exciting!

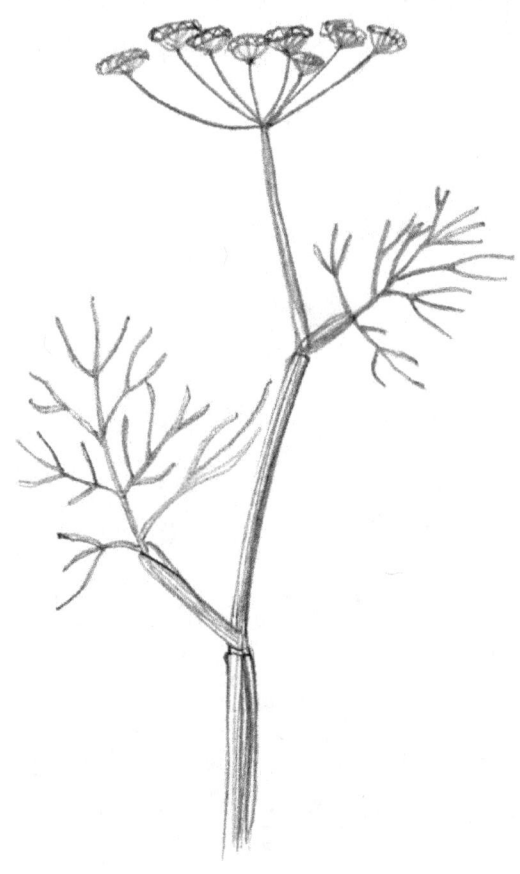

Picture 7. Weeping Petals

Here we have a plant that requires some excellent shading work and focus.

Start out by getting those thin lines drawn in for the stalk and the sprouts that are coming out of the side of the plants stalk. Then from there you will want to start drawing in the petals (a-d).

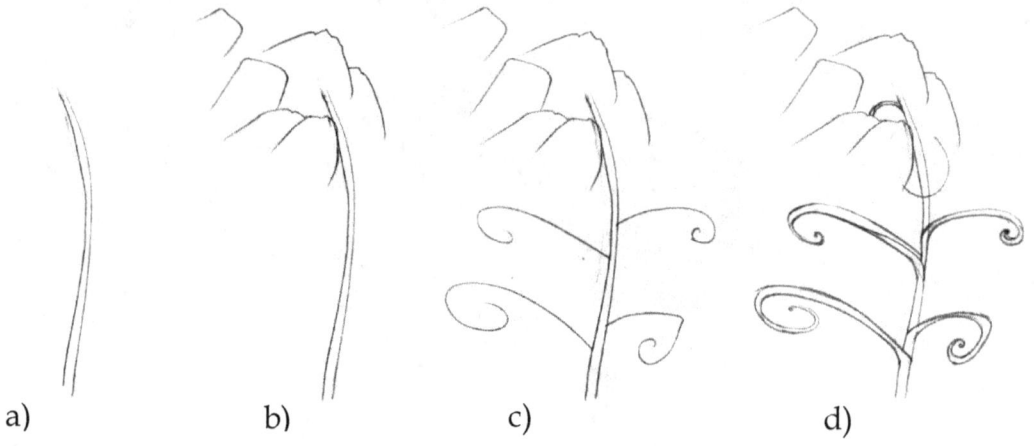

a) b) c) d)

Once you have the layering of the petals right you get to start shading in the stalk of the plant and the sprouts, then it gets exciting and we get to shade the petals in next (e, d).

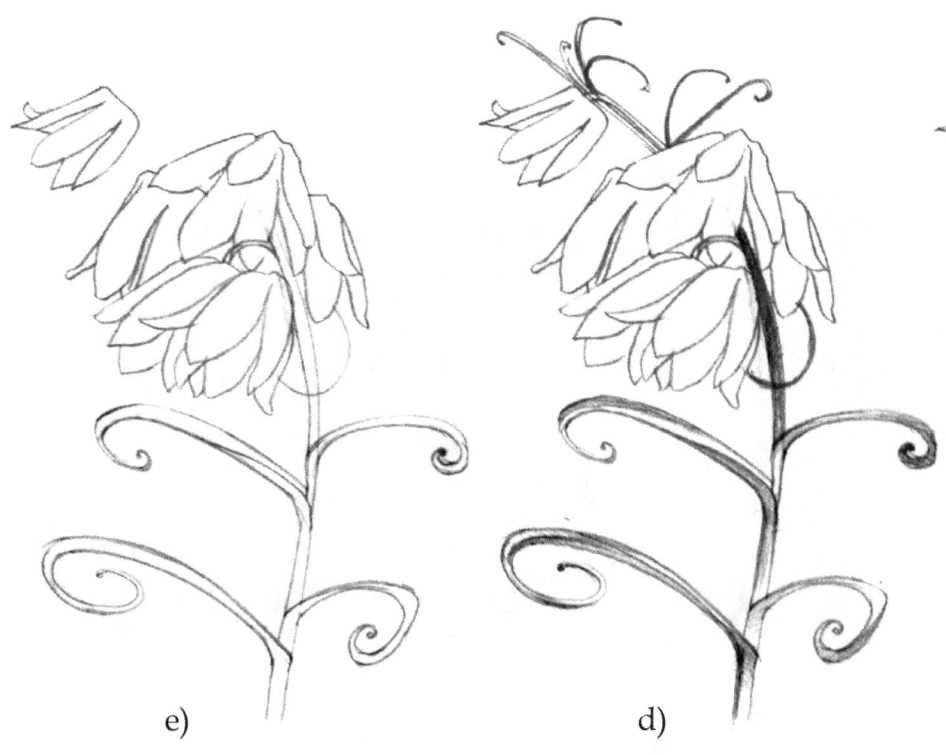

This drawing is excellent for shading as you get to see the way the layering of the petals affects the shading and then act accordingly on the rest of the plant.

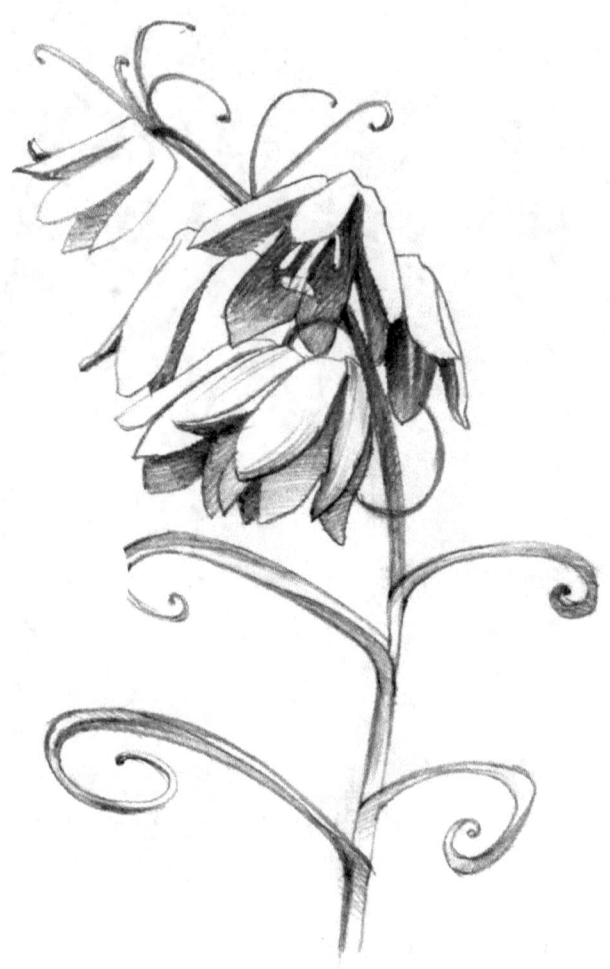

You can see that the tops of the petals have very delicate and soft shading but underneath is very dark and dense and the shading is thick as well. It's almost black when shaded. The detail on this plant is important too, the little sprouts and petals near the top, those aren't necessarily the focus of the image but they matter.

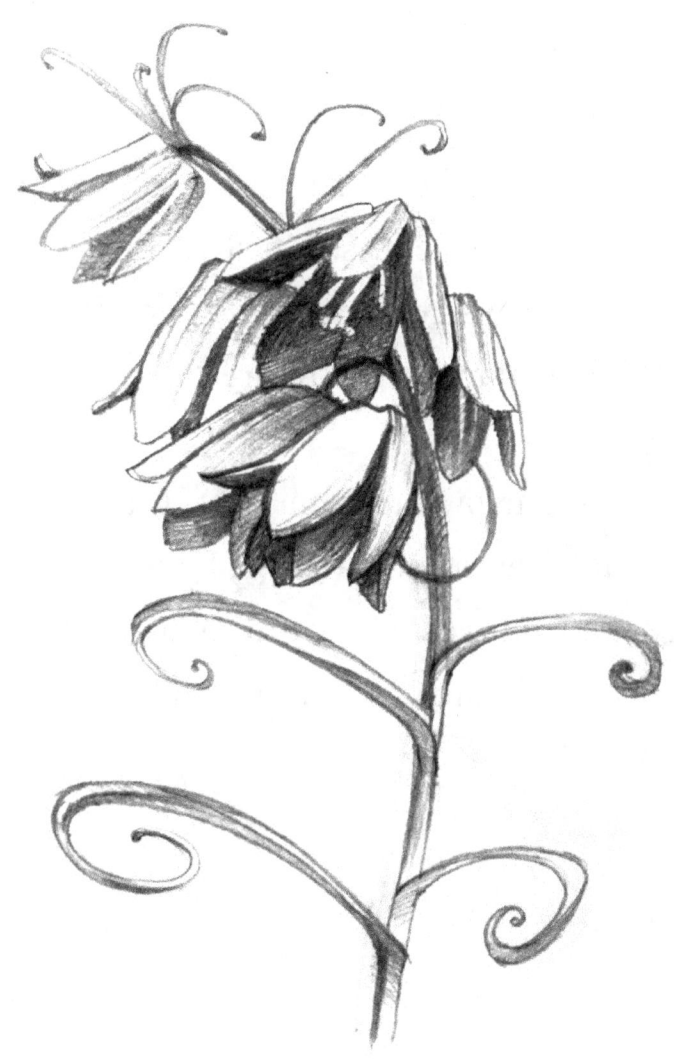

Finally you have a well shaded and well sketched flower. This is another example of planning the place of the light source before hand; take a second to think about how you would have shaded this one if the light source was in a different spot.

Picture 8. Pointed Leaves

This drawing is much different than the last two just primarily for the fact that if you didn't know any better it's completely shaded, and that is because it is. Which is an interesting way to approach this one? As well there are a lot finer details here in this image to respect and approach with care.

Start out with the narrow but firm lines of the stalks and then add on the pointed leaves and petals (a, b). Once those are added start shading them immediately with almost no concern for a light source, but make sure to pay attention to the way it's shaded in the image (c).

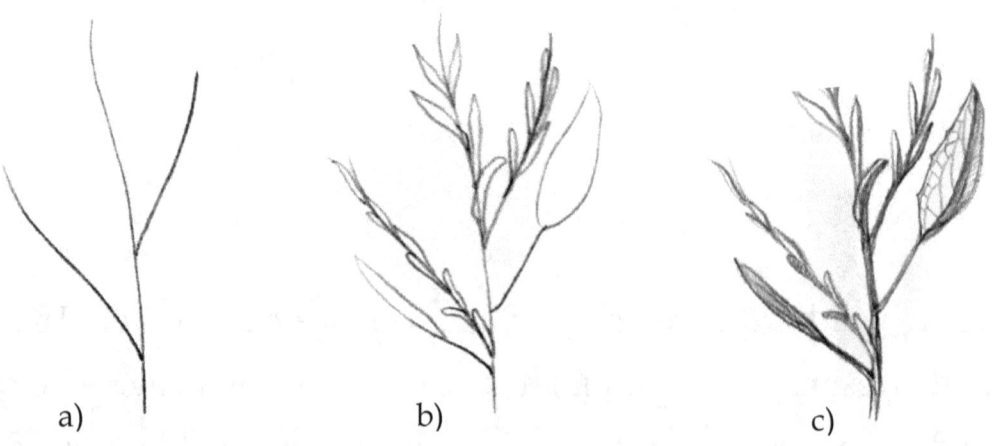

Once that is done you start adding the flowers on top of the stalks, two that have bloomed and one that hasn't.

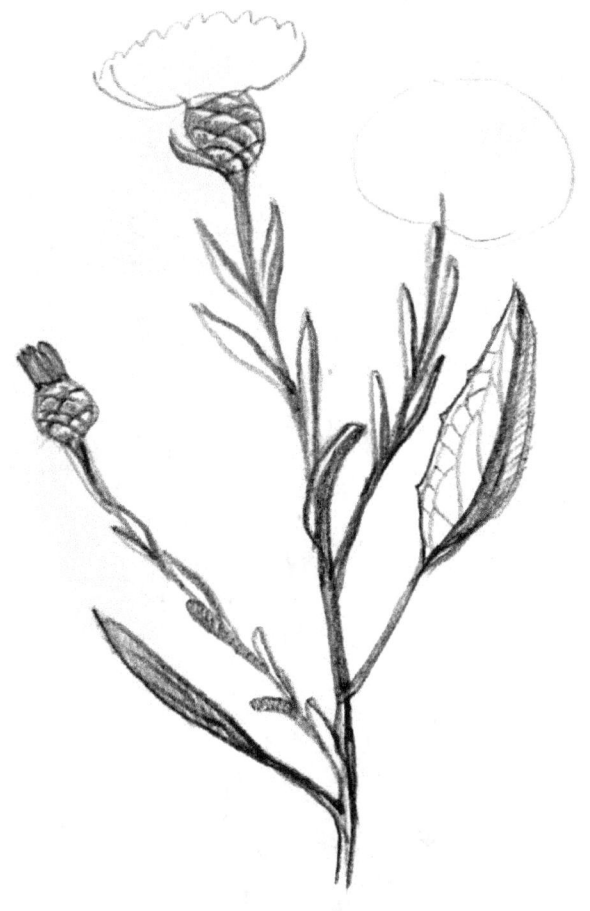

The final step is simply to add detail to the blossomed flowers with lots of little thin petals which are also shaded to start out with. This is an example of over utilizing shading for the sake of style. That isn't a bad thing. It can look really good like in this image, but you do need to be careful how often you utilize it and what you utilize it on.

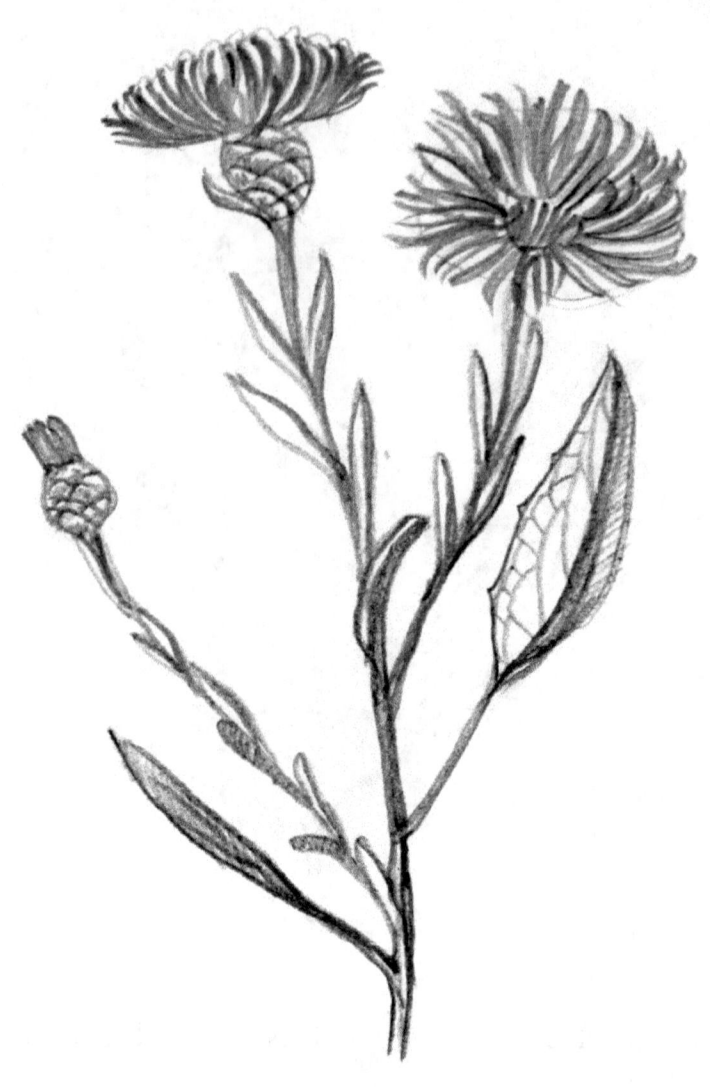

Picture 9. Small Flowers

Here we have another great example of an image that doesn't rely heavily on shading but relies very heavily on the detailing. Put the shading out of your mind for this one like the first one and make sure you follow the steps of the image carefully.

Start with the thin stalks, and then add the small flowers to them (a, b). You may need to look closely but the stalks of the flowers are fuzzy near the tops, you'll need to use small and precise lines to emulate that. Then make sure that the small leaves you add in on the bottom and near the top have a firm outline but softer interiors (c).

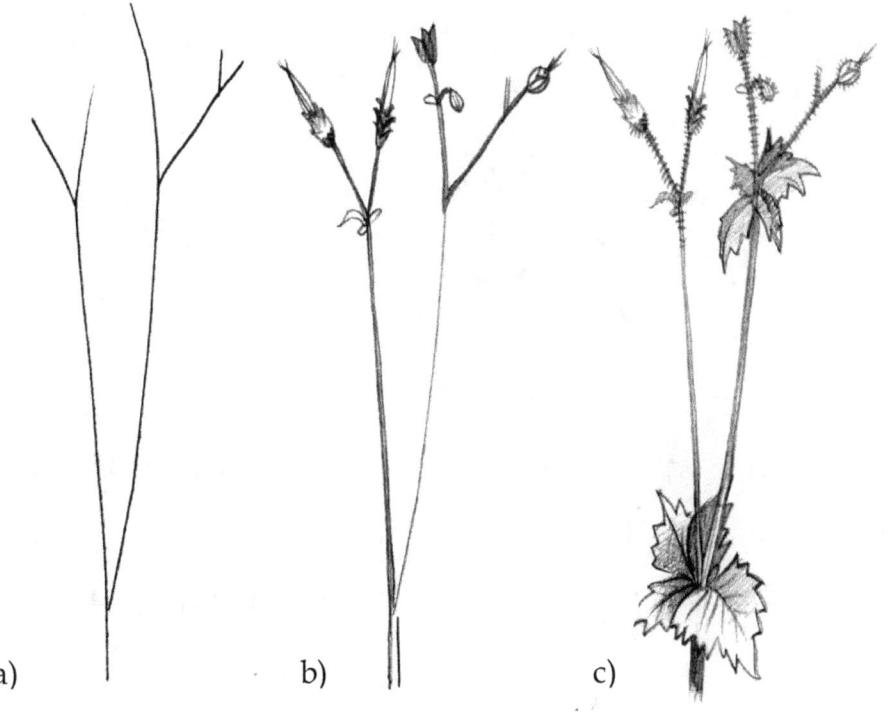

You'll also be adding in the flowers to the top of the plant as well, these have two tones in them with a very dark centre and then a lighter outer ring but white petal tips.

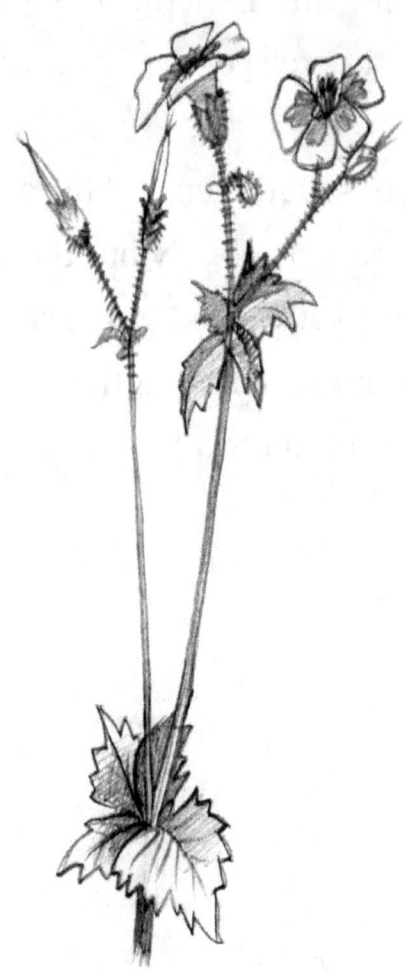

From there you will start on the big maple leaf in the middle. This is where the attention to detail and shading will need to come in and be of utmost importance to the image.

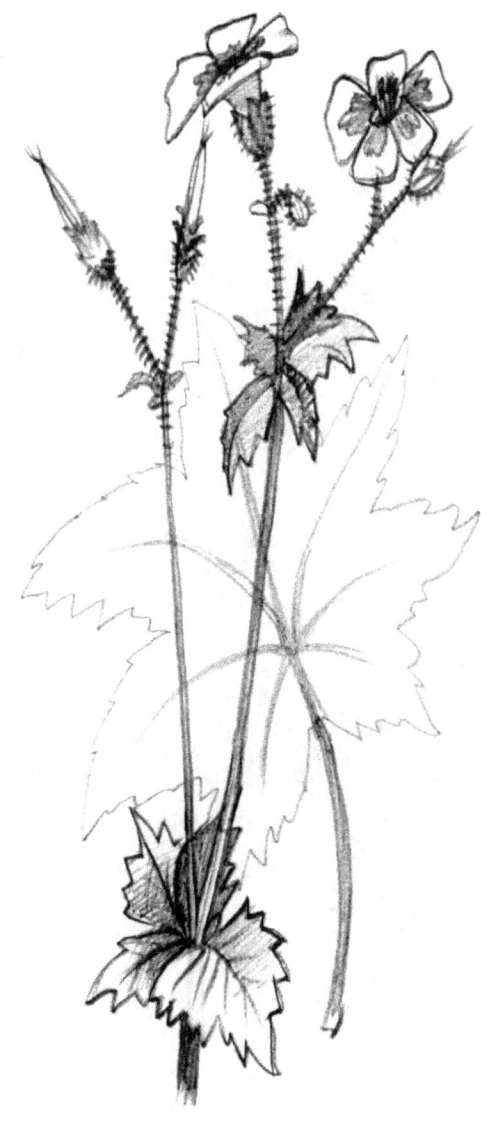

From the outline inward you want to be using softer shading but also make sure to darken the details where required, and you've completed the image.

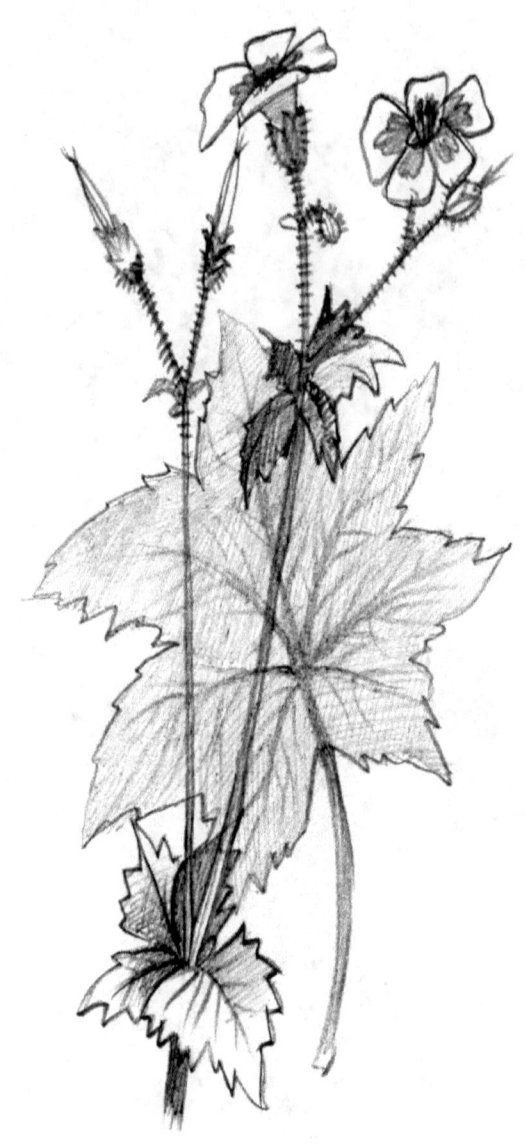

Picture 10. Pretty Petals

In what is quickly becoming a pattern of this section, we start out with some thin stalks that need no shading to start (a). Them we add on to the, with some small petals. You will also notice that fairly quickly we wind up thickening up the stalks so keep that in mind (b).

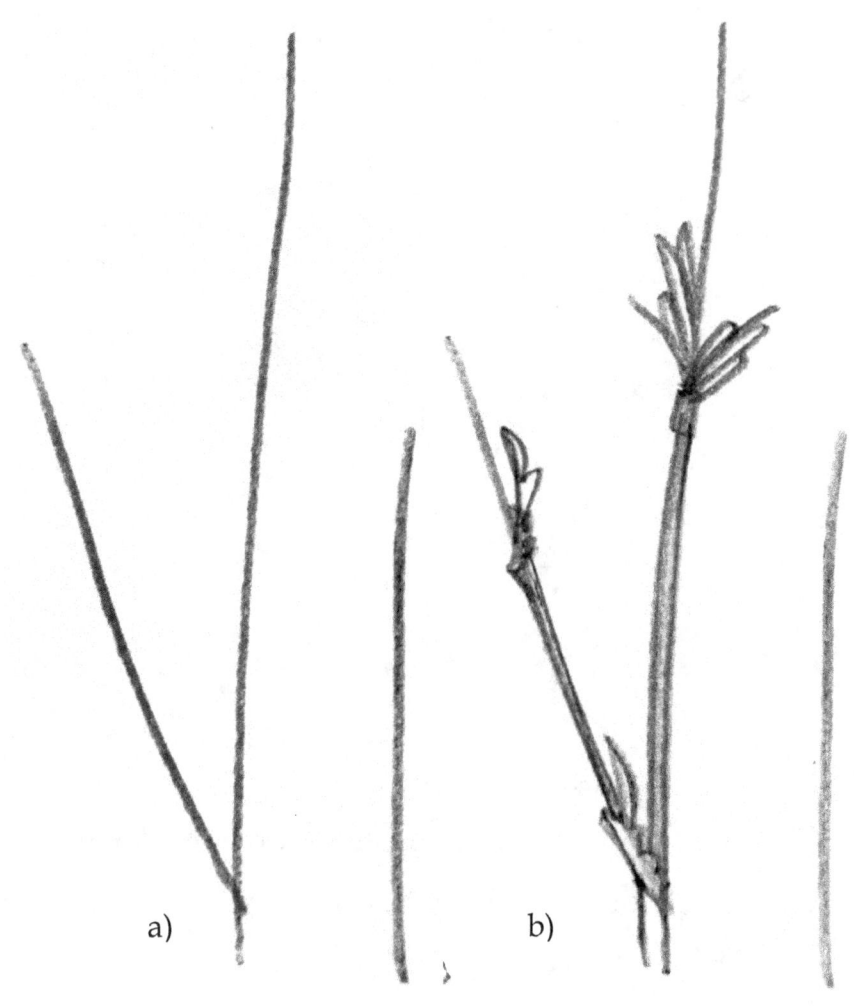

In the third step you will be adding the petals onto the stalks, small ones and large ones. These will be the focus of the image as you'll note in step five.

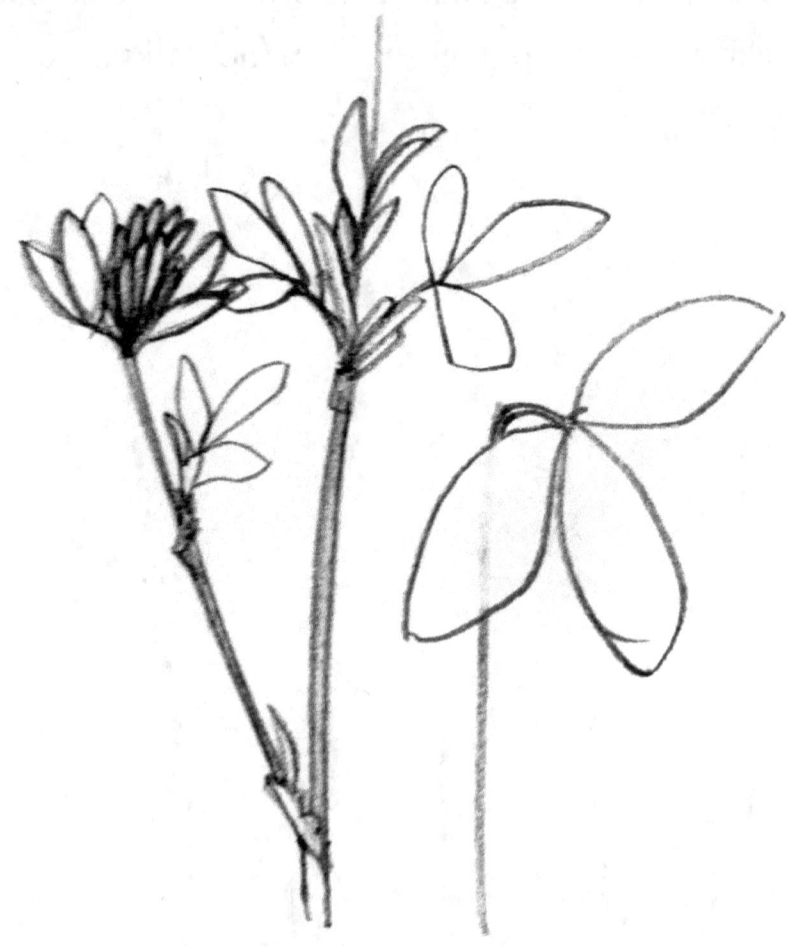

In the fourth step we add in two small flowers on the longer stalks. These two have some finite details with very light shading as seen in the fifth and final step.

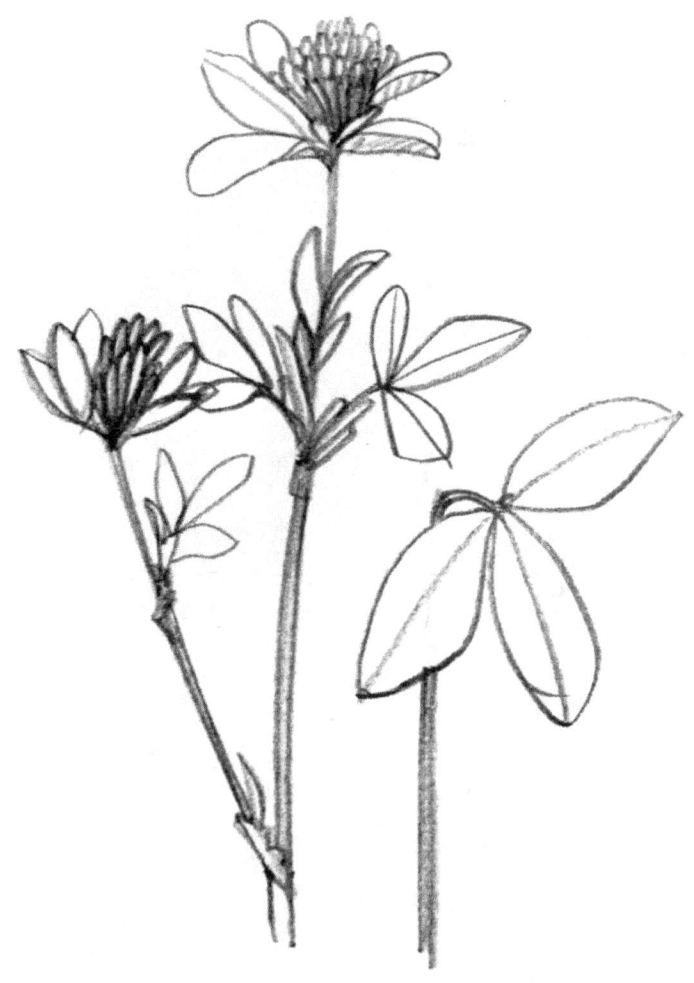

For the last step you will be sketching the pattern onto the petals that you see in the image. This is then when we start to shade in the petals. However you might notice that the only petals that have significant shading are indeed the larger ones that are closer to the front of the drawing.

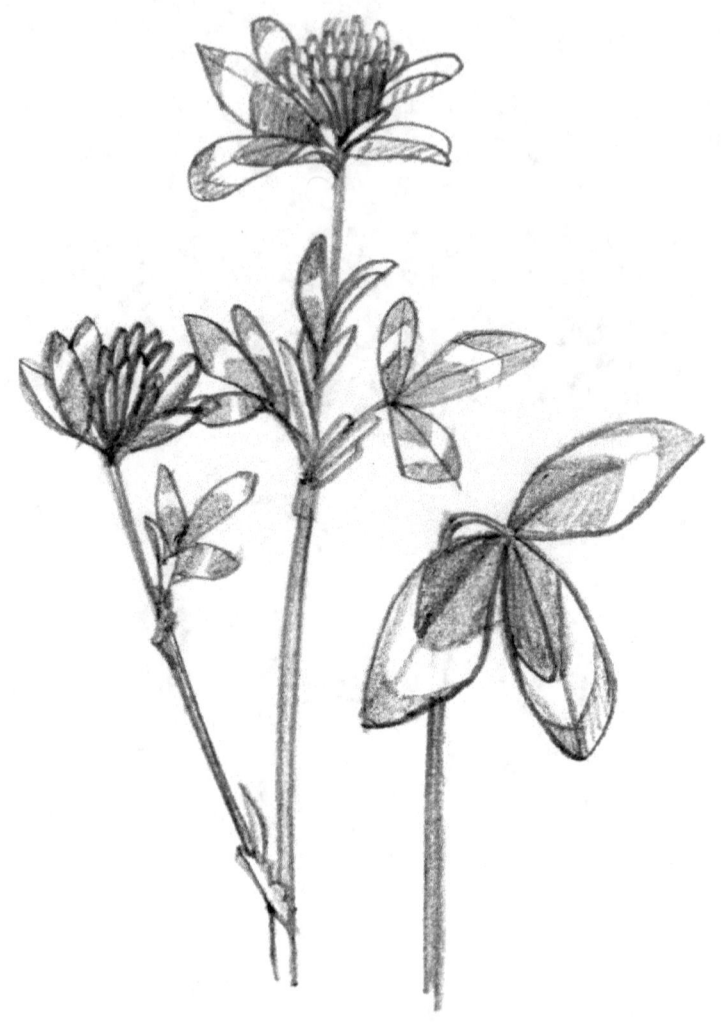

This is another fairly simple image in regards to detail. Yet think of it this way, if you added this drawing into any one of the animal drawings would that not be interesting and create something beautiful?

Picture 11. Simple Flower

Congratulations on reaching the halfway point in this section! That means you are that much closer to working on some gorgeous landscapes. Until then the task is this next flower at hand.

This flower combines a lot of the detail oriented flowers we've done with some of the more shading oriented ones we've done. The way to approach this one is slowly. Get that line work done on its stalk, petals and the flower itself and then start plotting the light source (a, b, c).

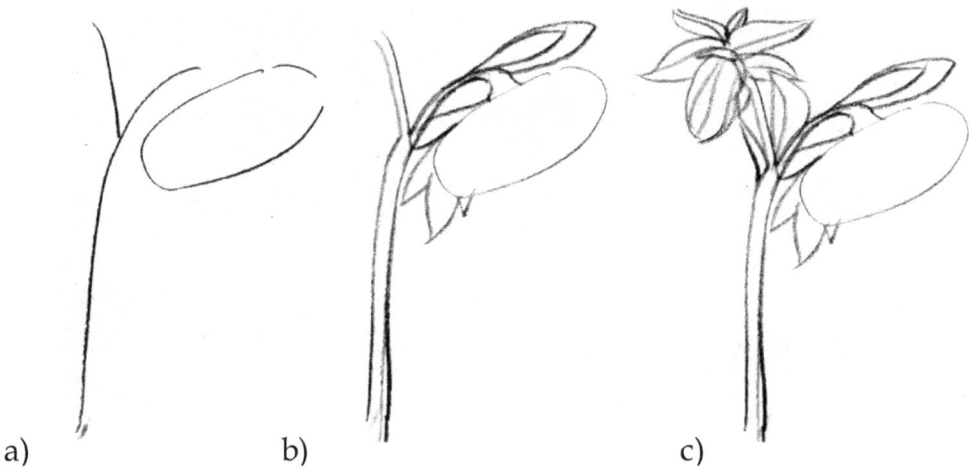

Once you figure out where the light is and the way it impacts the flower and all of its aspects you can start to think about actually shading it in (e).

Once you have addressed those thoughts it's time to start shading it in. You will notice that the stalk is shaded in darkly along one of the sides of it and all of the petals are shaded more underneath. In the flower it is most dark between the two top petals (d).

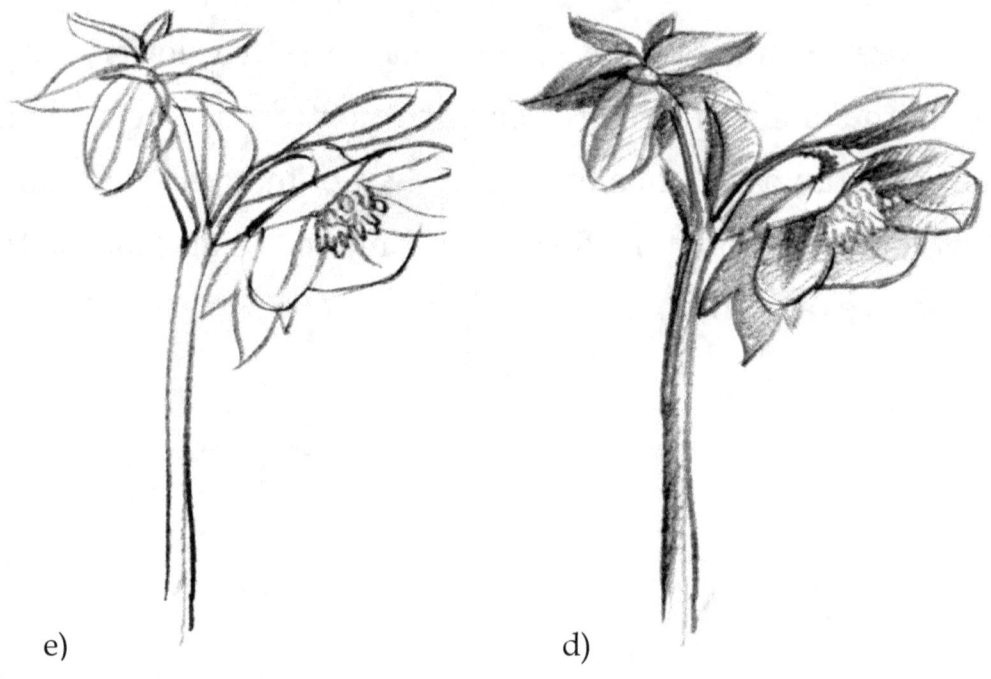

e)   d)

This makes sense and is a great way of dictating how the light affects the image.

Picture 12. Fanning Leaf

In the final stretch of this section you have another one that deals more with the shading than with the detail.

Do the line work for the stalks and then approach the next part carefully (a). You can see that there's what looks like a flower bulb or a rock and dirt at the bottom of the stalks (b). This is the element of the biggest detail in the image. Handle it with ease and precision and then move on to the next step.

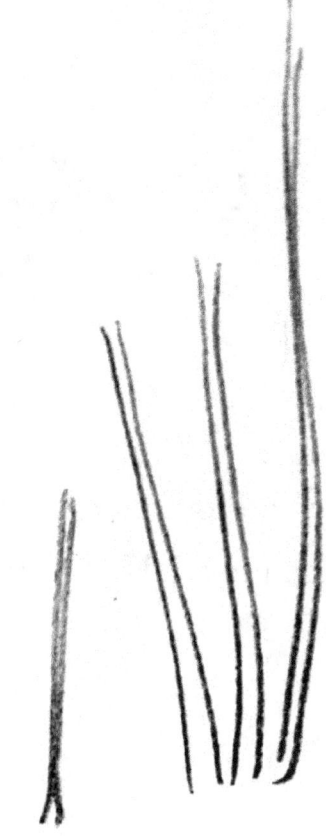

a)

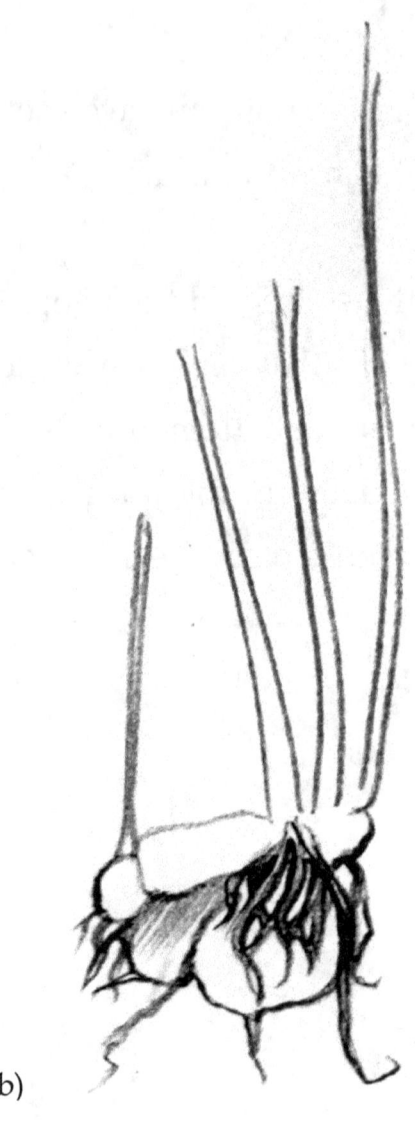

b)

This next step is the addition of all of the leaves and petals. Here we see some extra shading added to the portion at the bottom of the image.

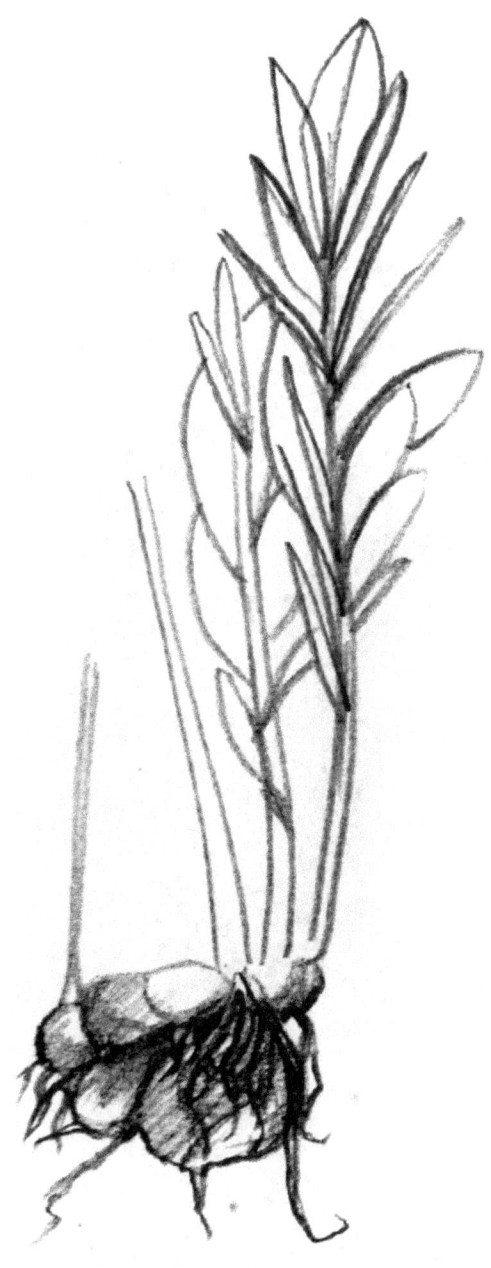

Next up we fill in the rest of the leaves on the last two stalks on the left hand side.

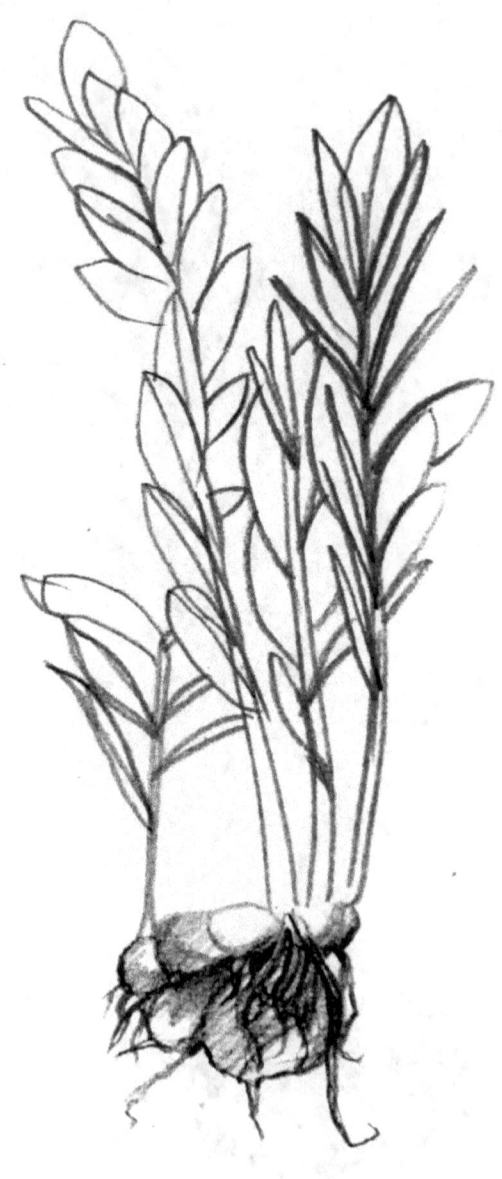

This brings you to the fifth and final step which focuses on shading all of the areas not shaded yet, like the leaves and the stalks. The darkest set of shading is the stalk and the leaves at the very back of the image, which could mean that they are shaded by some of the leaves and stalks that are ahead of it.

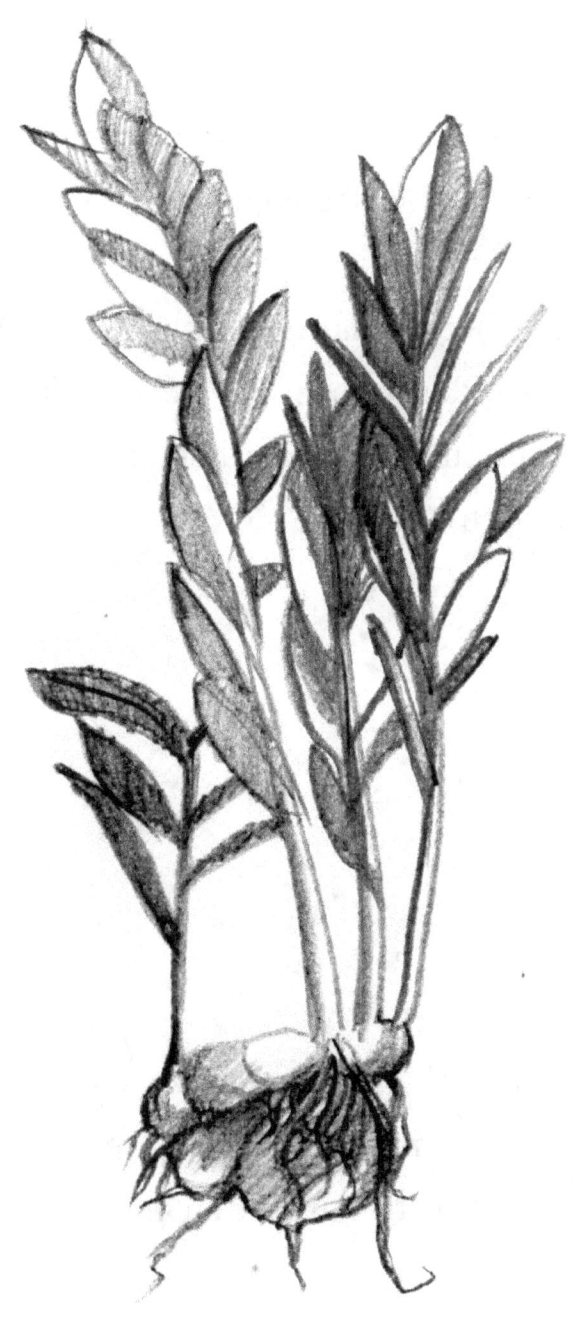

Picture 13. Rose and Leaves

This image goes back to focusing more on the actual detail in shading and not just overall shading.

The main drawing here is fairly simple, with lots of different petals that overlap and layer over one another (a). You also need to pay attention to the fact that there are two roses in this combination as well (b).

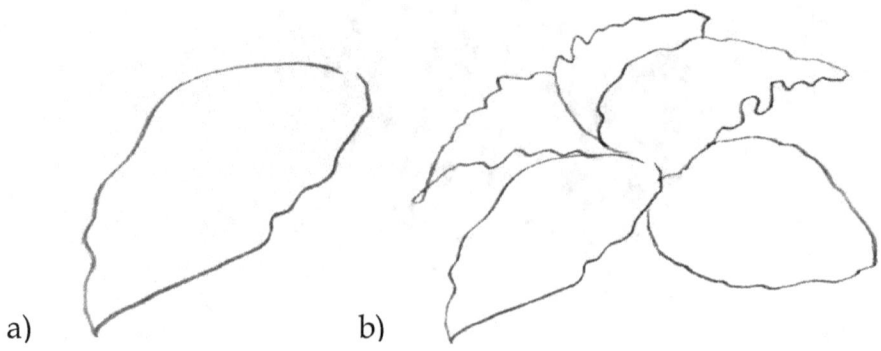

a)   b)

Layer the leaves properly and then make sure that the petals of the roses are drawn in carefully and also layered nice and equally. From there you are ready to start adding the detail.

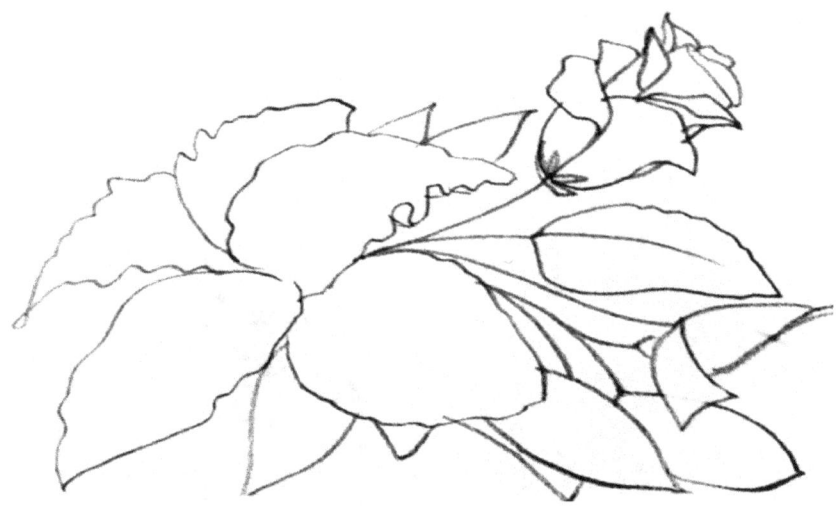

The detailed shading is most complex on the petals of the rose above the other one, and then the leaves on the left hand side. The rest is fairly straightforward but you still need to watch out for the extremities, such as underneath each petal there's some falling shadow that overlaps other leaves that you need to watch out for.

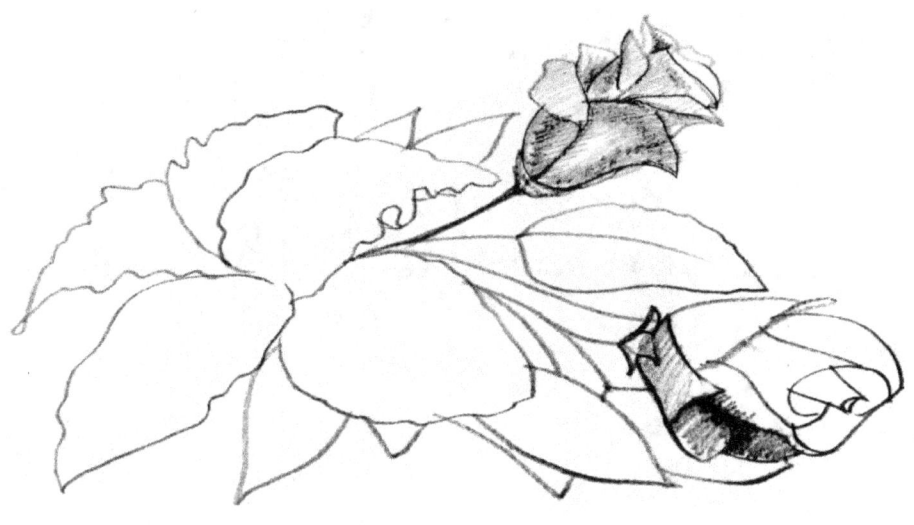

As a closing note you will want to utilize the blending skill in this scenario as well to really give a smooth and soft feel to the beauty of the image.

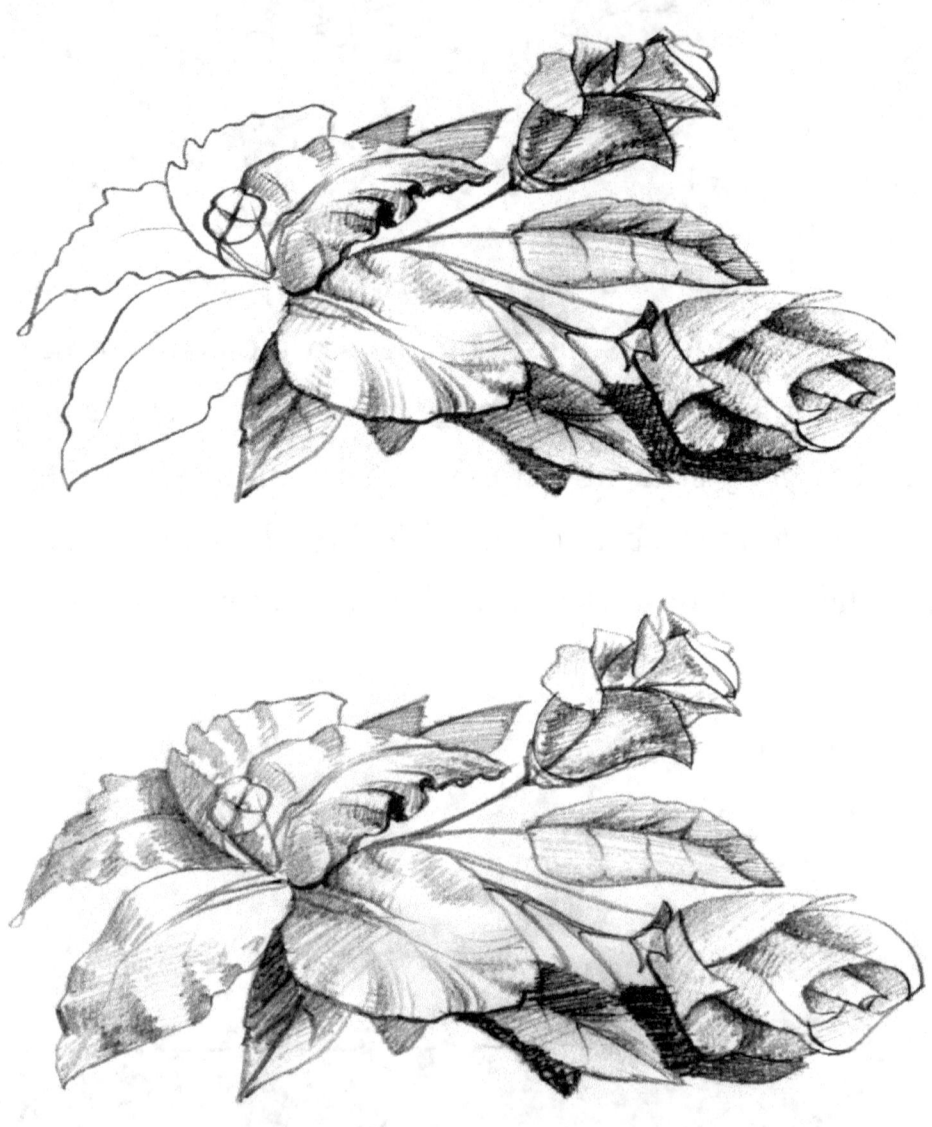

Picture 14. Bouquet

Third to last image and we are faced with some serious shading. There isn't a lot of shading in this image specifically but there is definitely some heavy shading done where it is being used.

Start out with the stalk of the flower, and then make sure to draw the flower off shoots and the small petals as well as seen in the second step (a, b).

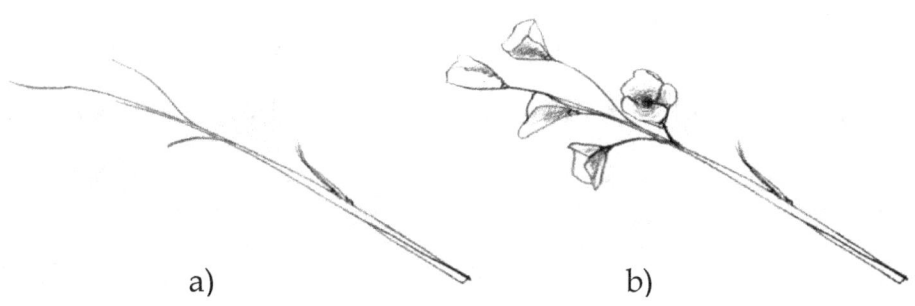

The third step brings in the bigger petals or the lower flowers and also shows some light shading on the petals of the upper flowers.

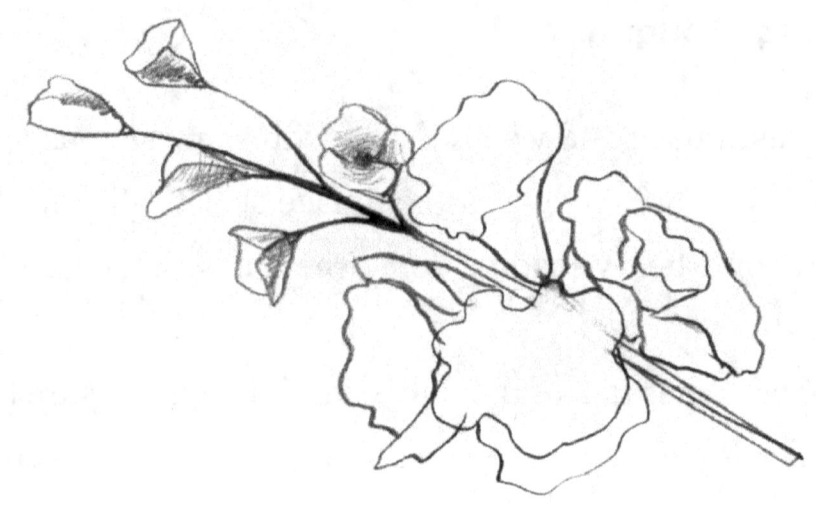

The fourth step we add the final details to flowers and then shade them in. The shading here is mostly light but very effective, giving the image a very third dimensional look to it and feel as well.

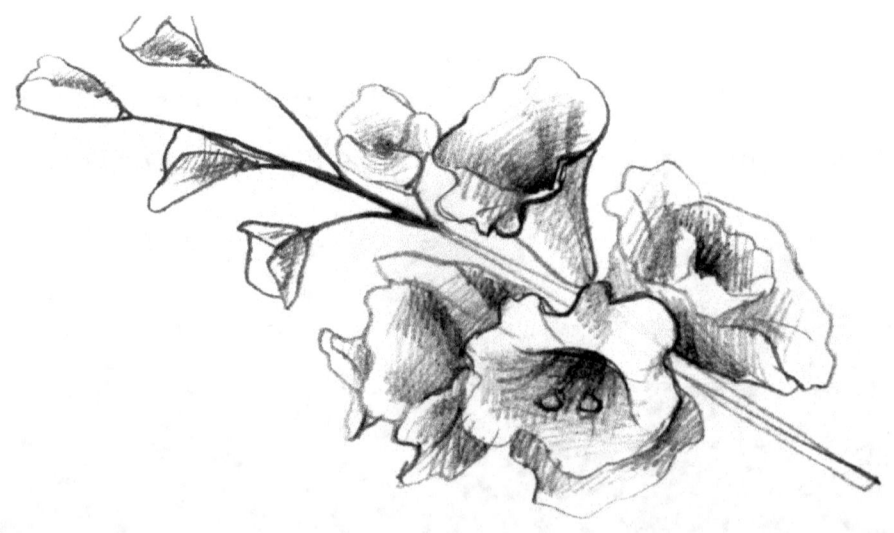

After that we approach the final step which is mostly just darkening the most extreme instances of the shading that pre-exist. Make sure to look the image over a couple times before calling it done to make sure that you've narrowed these segments down and really texturized them.

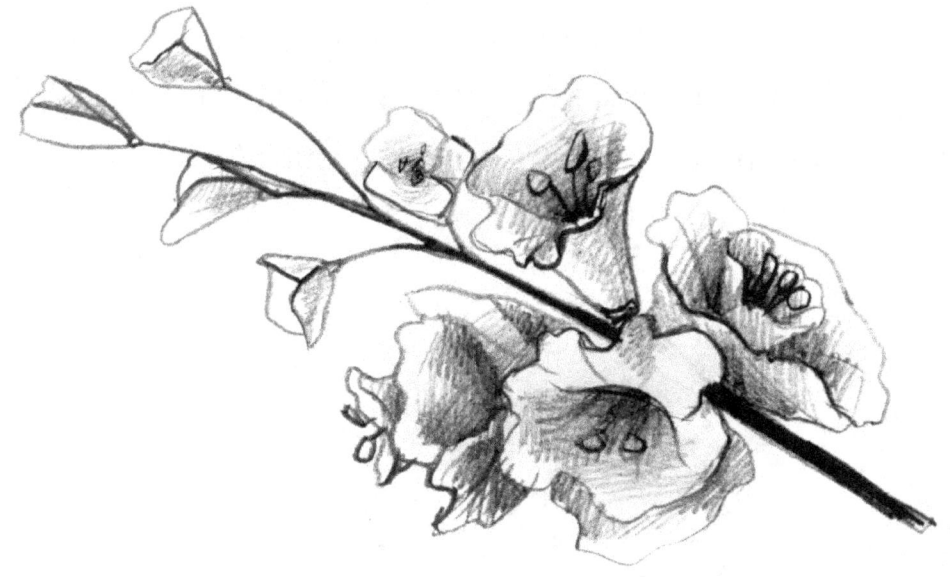

Trees

Picture 15. Basic Tree

This next drawing is an answer to the question "How do I shade a tree's many leaves?" Well here you go.

The easiest part is drawing the tree itself, and then from there the rest is all entirely shading and texturing (a). The leaves themselves can best be explained as like clouds (b).

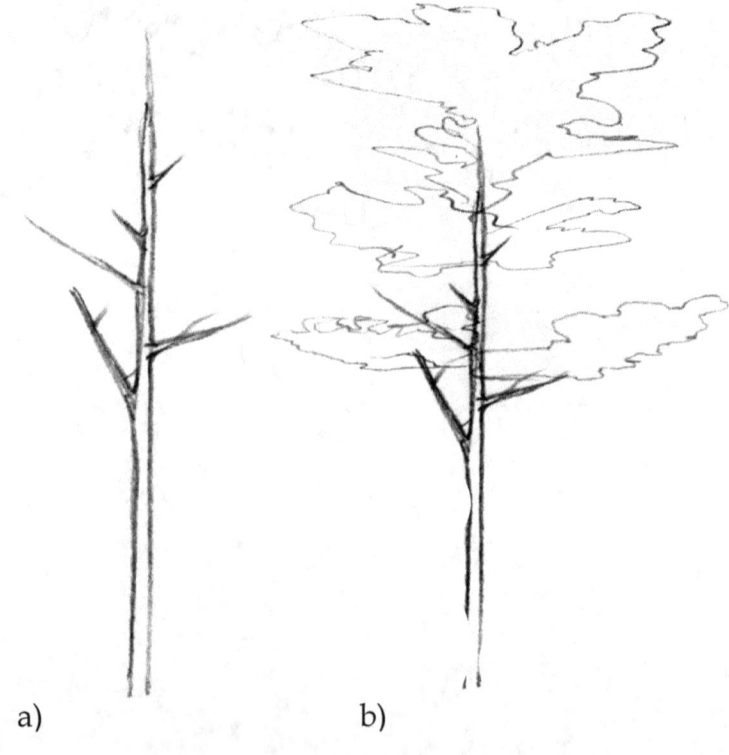

a) b)

Add in this cloud like entity on top of the branches that you drew in the first step, as seen above. Then once you have them in the formation and shape that you wanted them in you can start planning your shading.

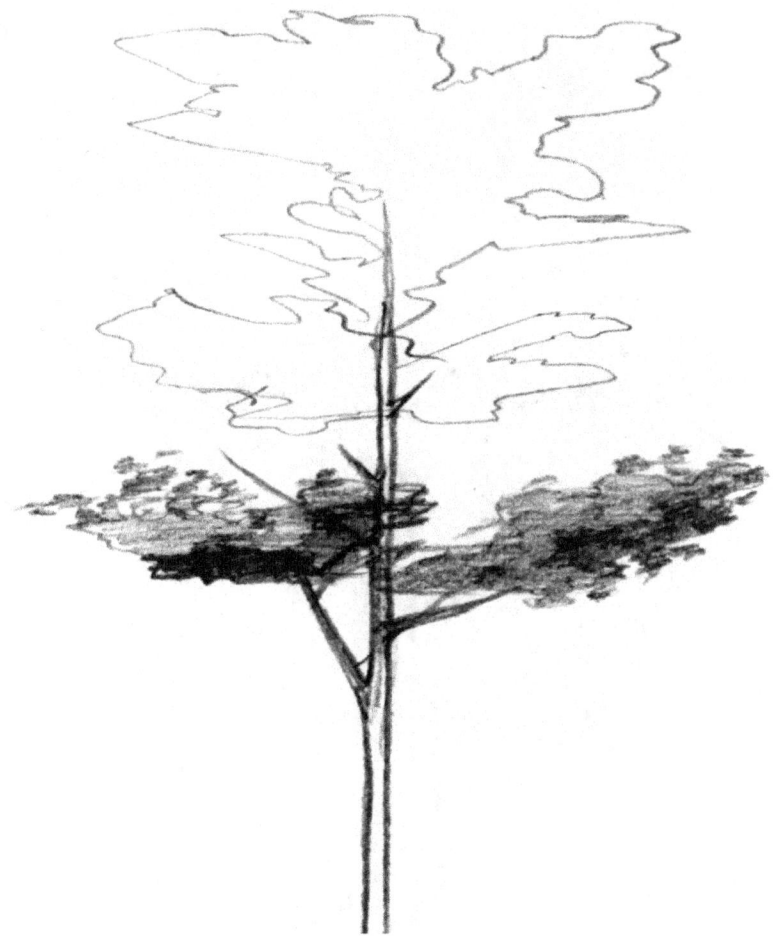

Assume that the light source is coming from the top left, and then you can move forward with the drawing. Shade all of the leaves with their own shade, so however dark the leaves are naturally, and then start working the shade from the light in.

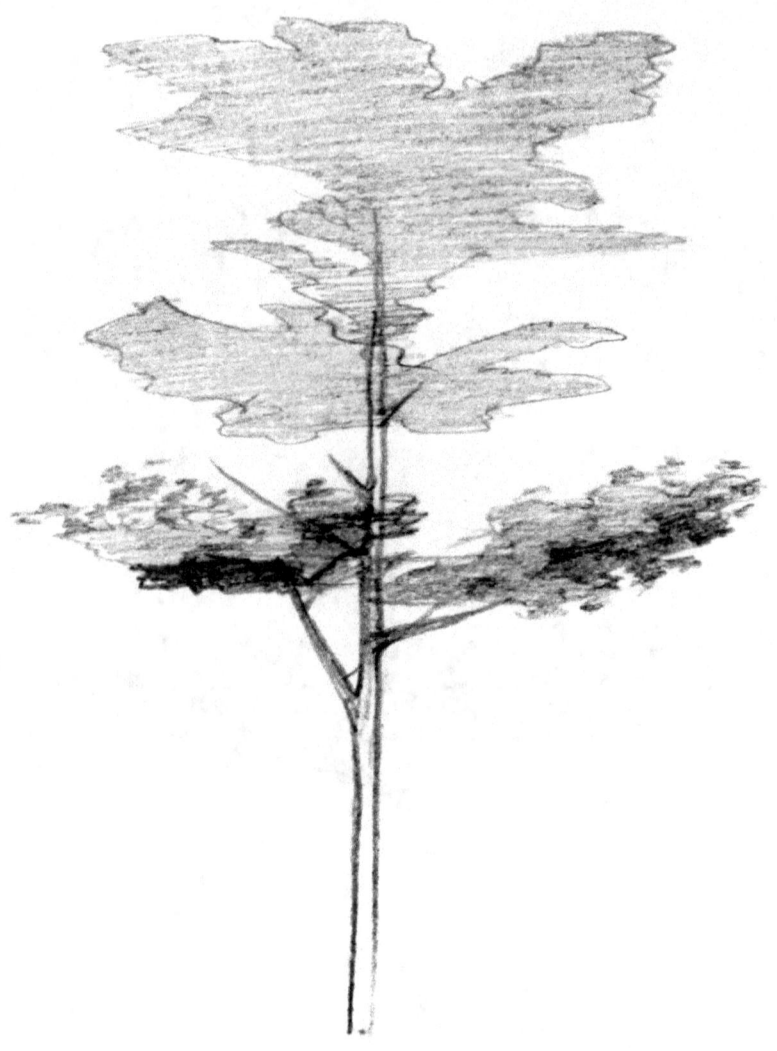

In this instance, the underneath of these leaf clouds is the darkest shading. The texturing here is important as well, you can see that it's mostly back and forth but feel free to experiment with different kinds.

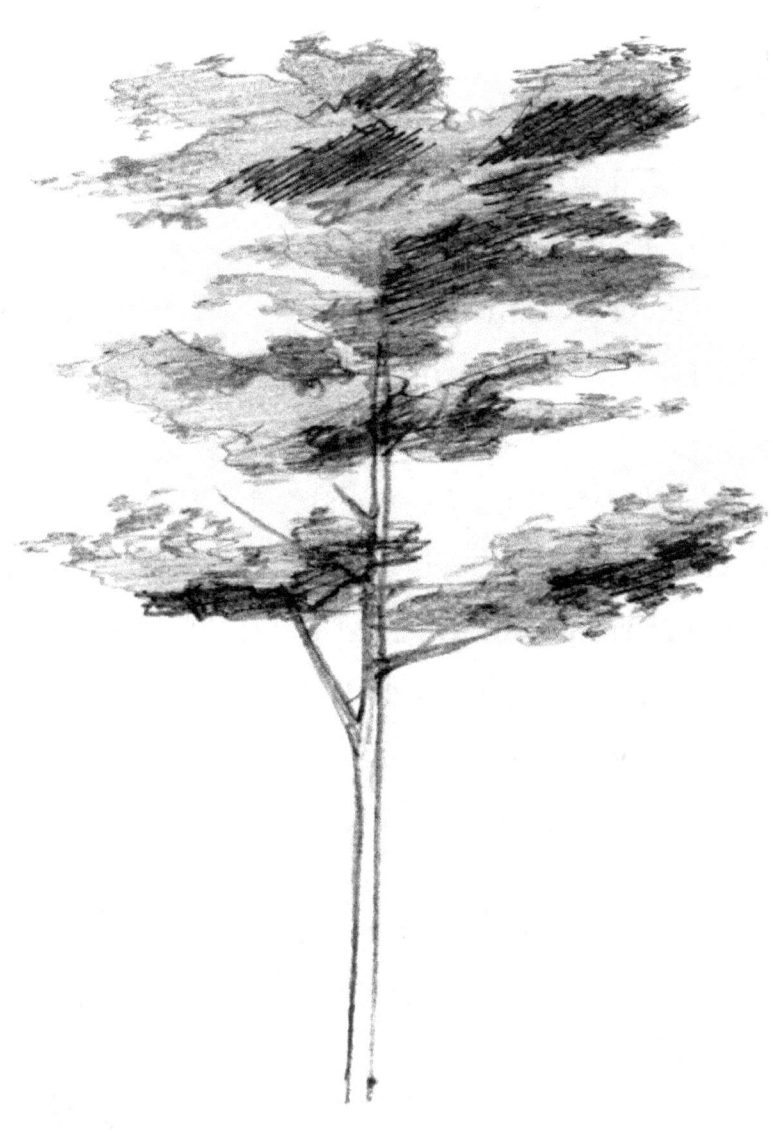

Picture 16. Leafy Tree

In what is probably the most complicated image in this section yet we have our first contact with a tree. This is in fact a palm tree. This kind of tree has very elaborate leaves and an almost even more elaborate trunk. The texture on the trunk will be a point of focus that you will want to approach carefully.

Start out with the trunk of the tree as seen above and then move on to the leaves (a, b). The leaves start out incredibly rough and just an outline. From there we start to add in the other elements of the leaves such as the short stalks that stick out of the top of the trunk, this is where the leaves grow from (c).

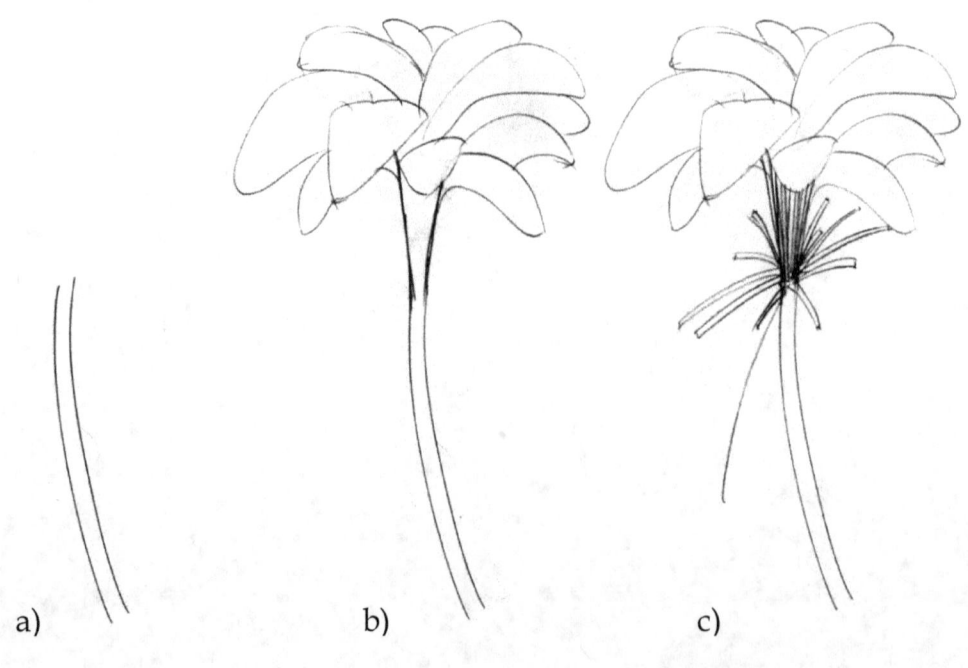

Then as you see in the fourth step we add in a couple leaves that are textured and shaded. These are slightly tricky but mostly there just require back and forth shading and texturizing.

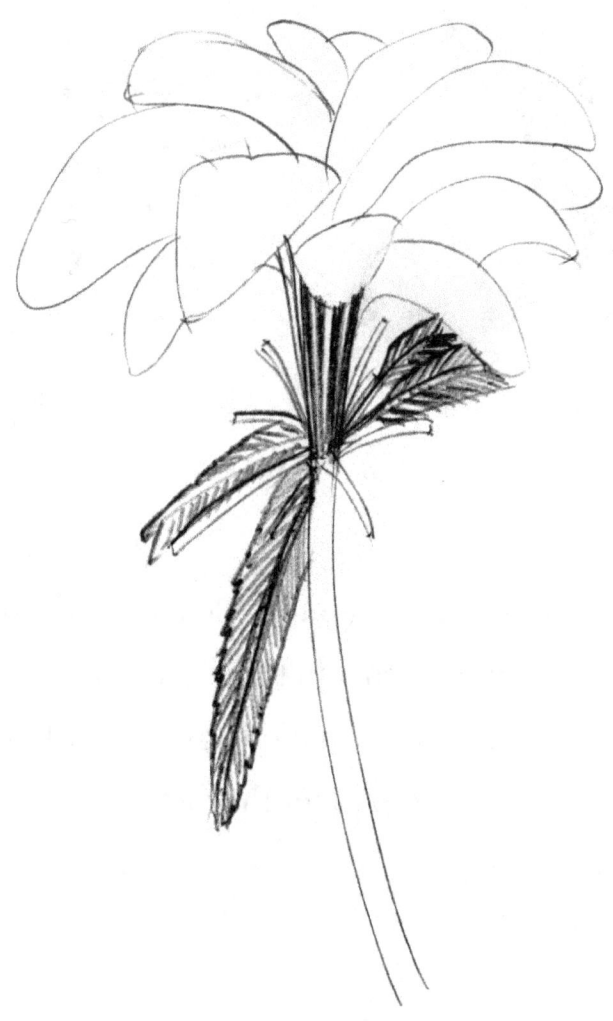

The trunk is the next part and this is essentially one giant and loose cross hatch from bottom to top (d). Do this and make sure to keep it consistent so it looks real (e).

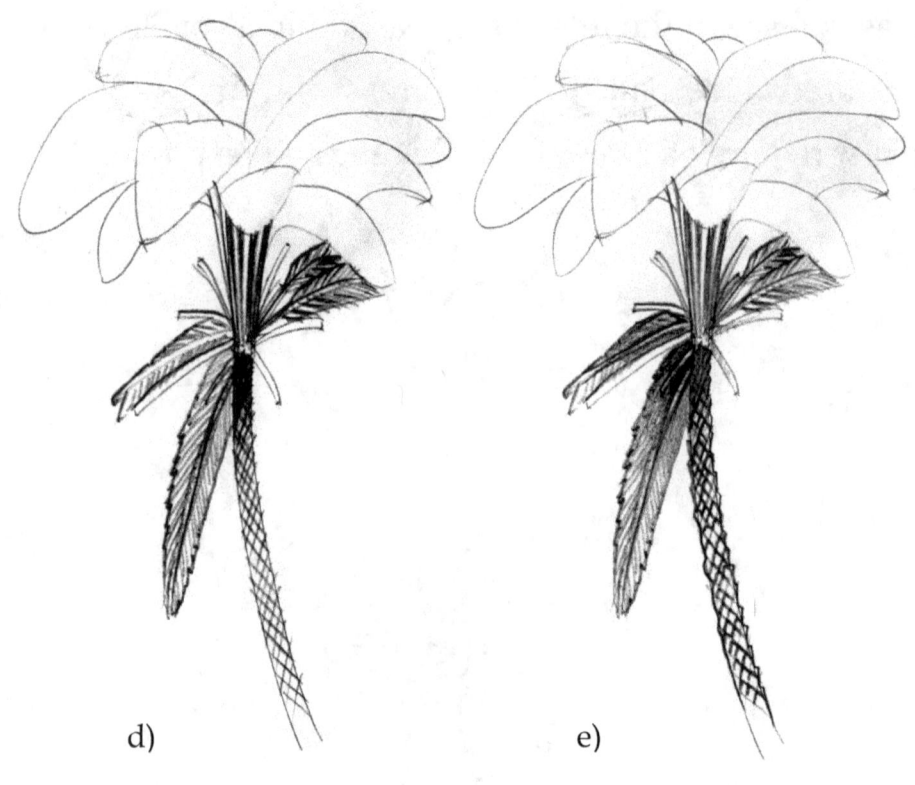

Them put your attention back on the leaves and do as described above to all of them, and then you'll see the way the lighting plays with the way the leaves are shaded (f). Use what you learned from the practice images to perfect the design (g).

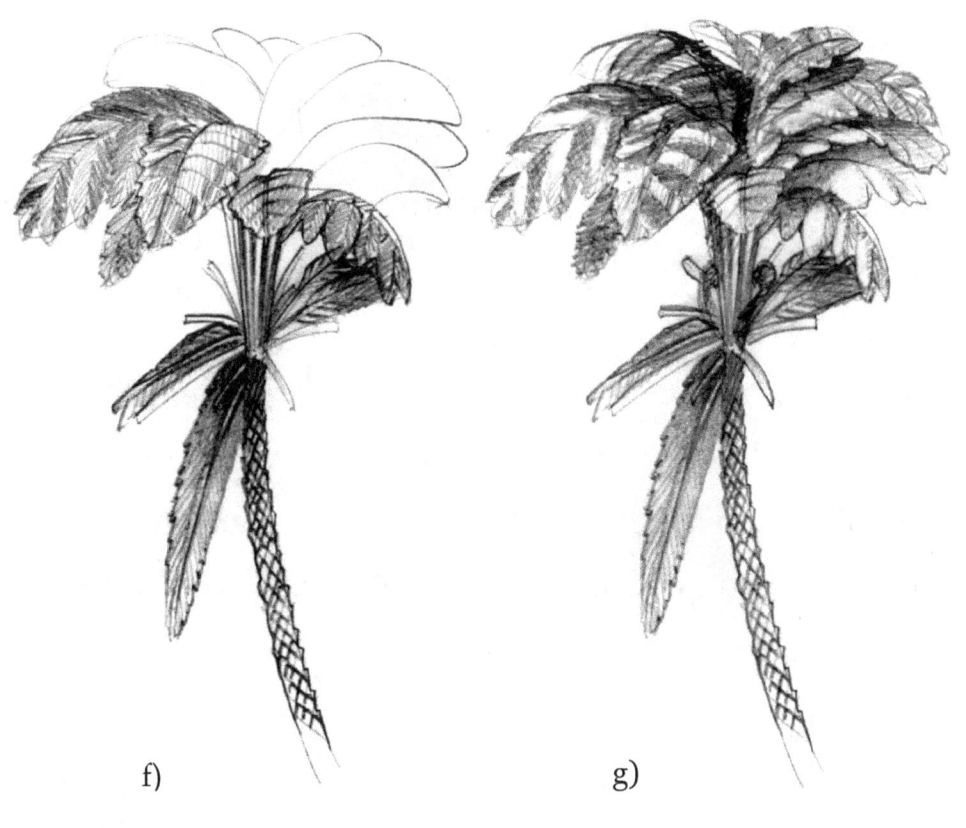

Picture 17. Tall Palm

This is the second occurrence of a palm tree which is advantageous because you can utilize the knowledge you gained from drawing the first one into this one.

Start out with the lines for the trunk and the outlines for the branches and leaves at the top (a, b). Right away we start detailing those branches with the leaves (c). You can see that its simple hatch-work, and then we shade that in for the next step and make it look nice and full as well as layered (d).

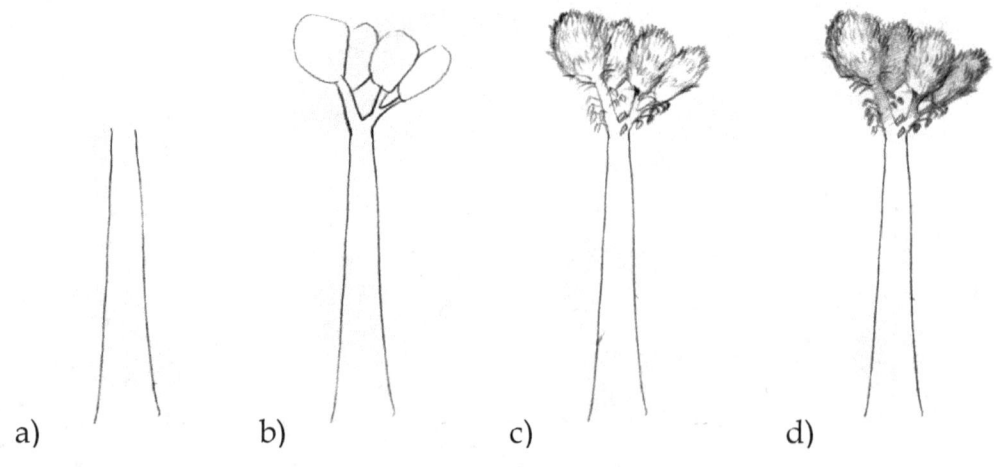

a)   b)   c)   d)

The next step sees us finally filling in the trunk of the tree, this is a good place to use the back and forth style of texturing to get that nice weathered look to the trunk. It makes for a very realistic layered look to it.

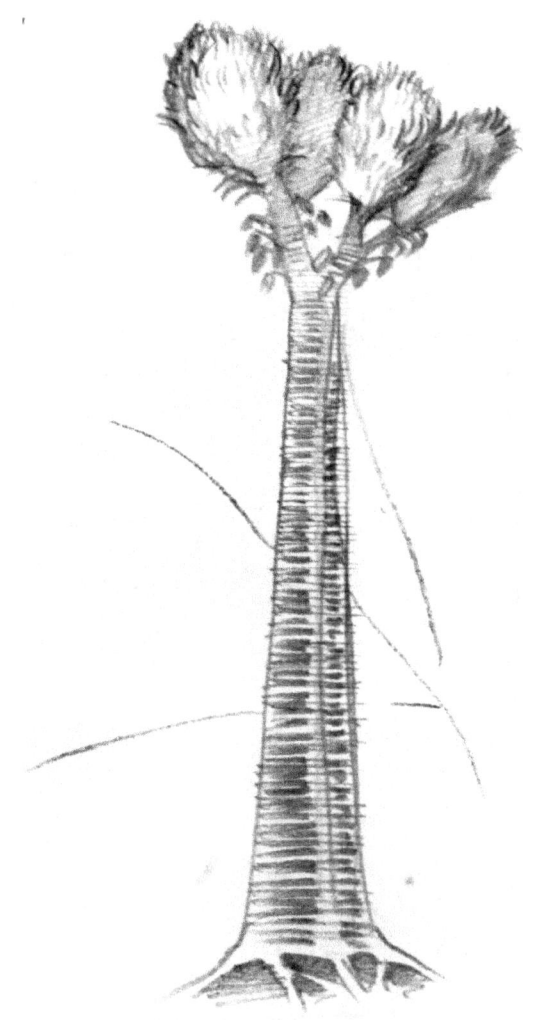

As well notice that the bottom of the trunk has some light root detailing to make it look like the ground is there as well (d).

Another interesting thing about this image is that there is a background. A leaf is added in here as a textured background for intrigue, this is a very simple leaf shaded which is barely shaded but the background itself is shaded very well (e).

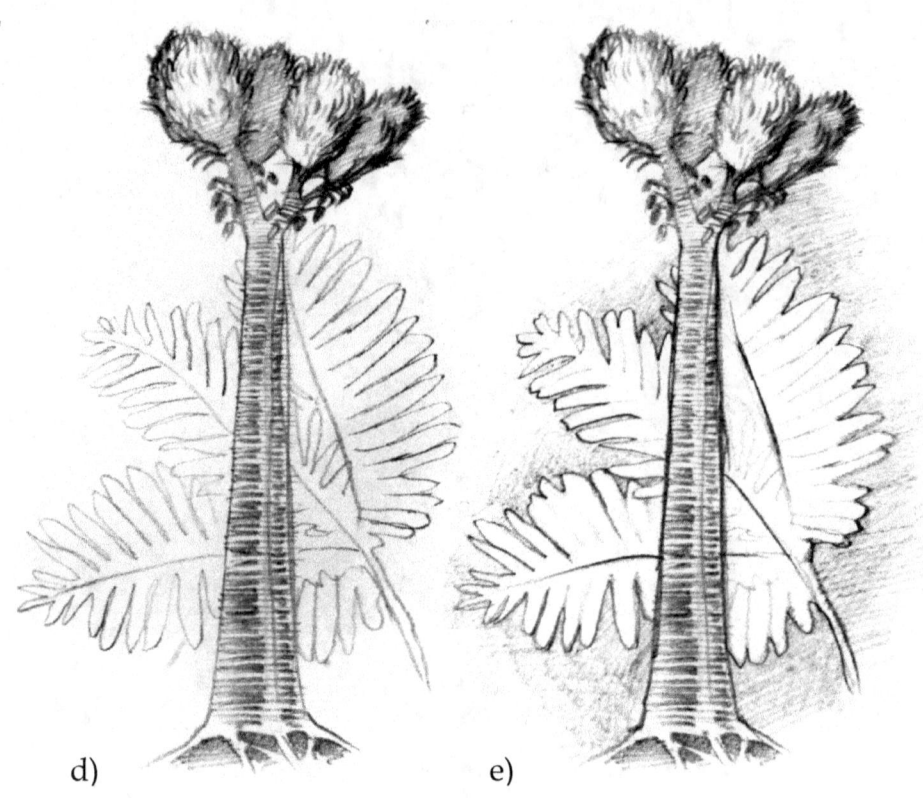

Picture 18. Thin Branched Tree

This image might be the easiest in the entire book, however there is something very special about it as well.

It isn't just easy, but it's important because it uses a form of shading we haven't explored yet. It uses shading without an outline. This image has you shade with no discernible outline, just the one you see in your mind.

Start out by drawing the thin but firm and heavy lined branches that go straight up (a). Darken them with some shading as well, and then let's talk about this new and very interesting form of shading (b, c).

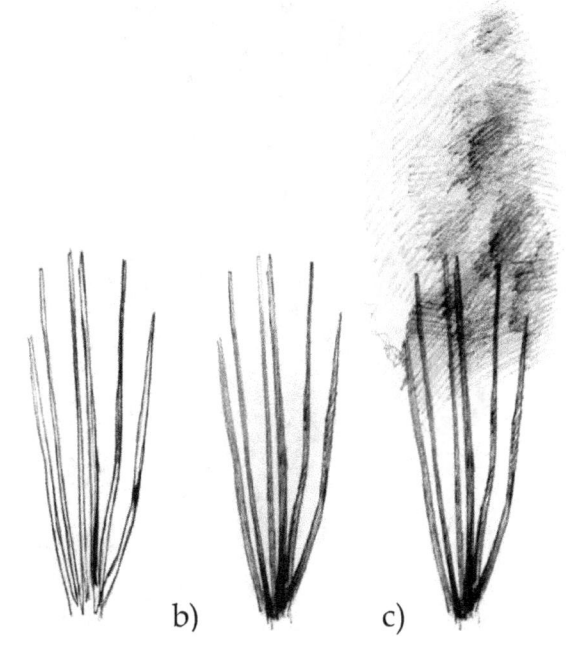

With this shading what you will want to do is definitely pre plan your light source and then approaches the image from a specific standpoint. The standpoint of knowing what you want from it. As you can tell by the final step in the image what we want is a very full looking tree with full bushels of leaves.

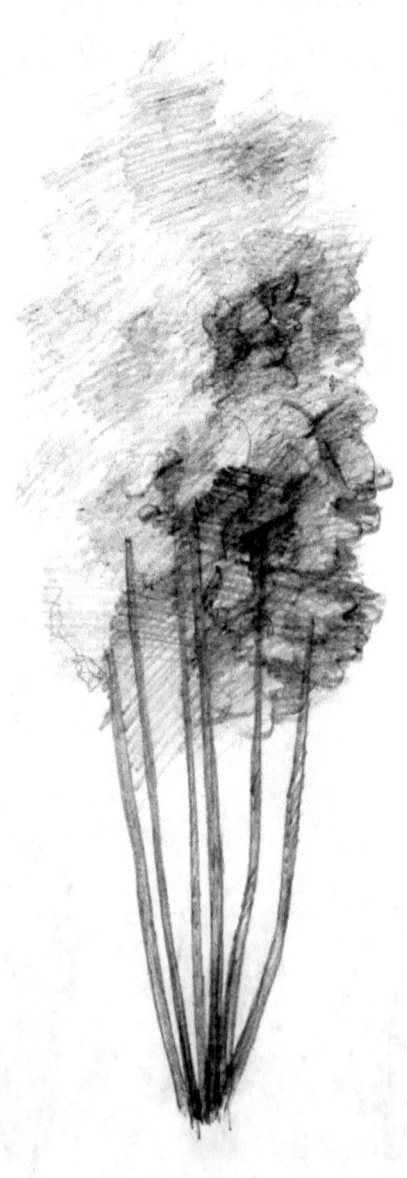

To do that you start out delicate and just use the back and forth texture to shade in from the branches and upwards, remembering to keep it light where the light source is. The next step is to keep layering it in only the areas that need to be darkened.

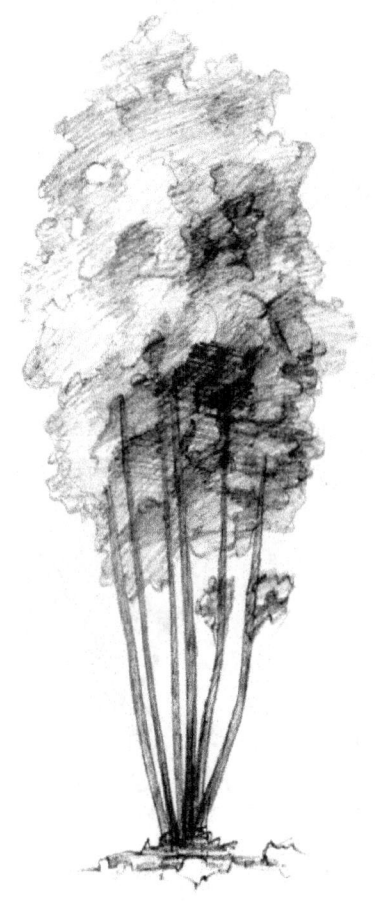

That is how you use this form of shading to your advantage; it's great for creating depth and texture without an outline.

Picture 19. Basic Tree Part 2

This is the very last and final image in the flower section. Ironically it is a tree as well, which is perfectly fine and acceptable. As well it's a very fun way to finish the section because this tree specifically is a great combination of all the skills you've learnt thus far in this book!

Move on with the drawing of the trunk (a). Shade it in, darkest at the top and then work your way down slowly softening the shading until you reach the bottom (b).

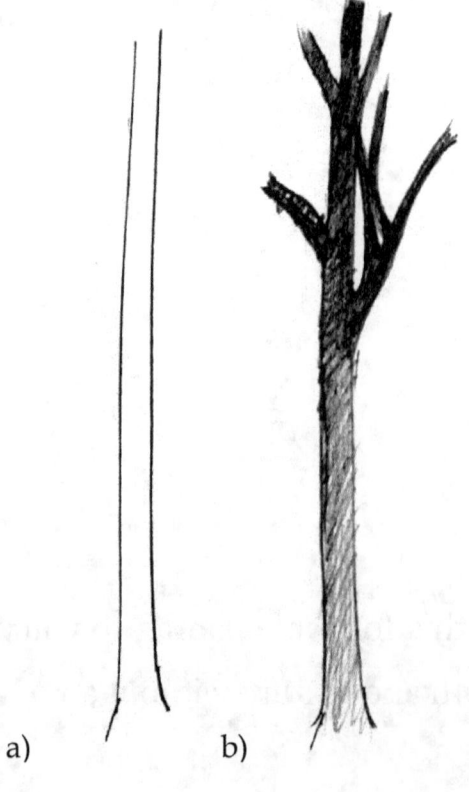

Then from there outline what will become the leaves and branches.

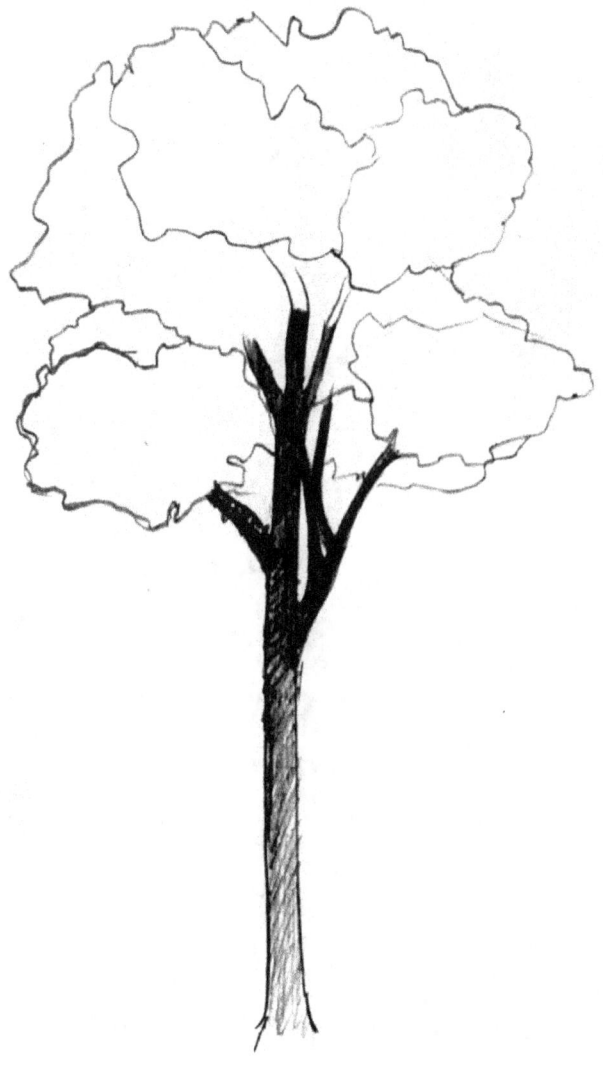

Once outlined shade within the outlines to create the texture and color you want for the leaves on their own insistence. From there you get to make the rest of the choices.

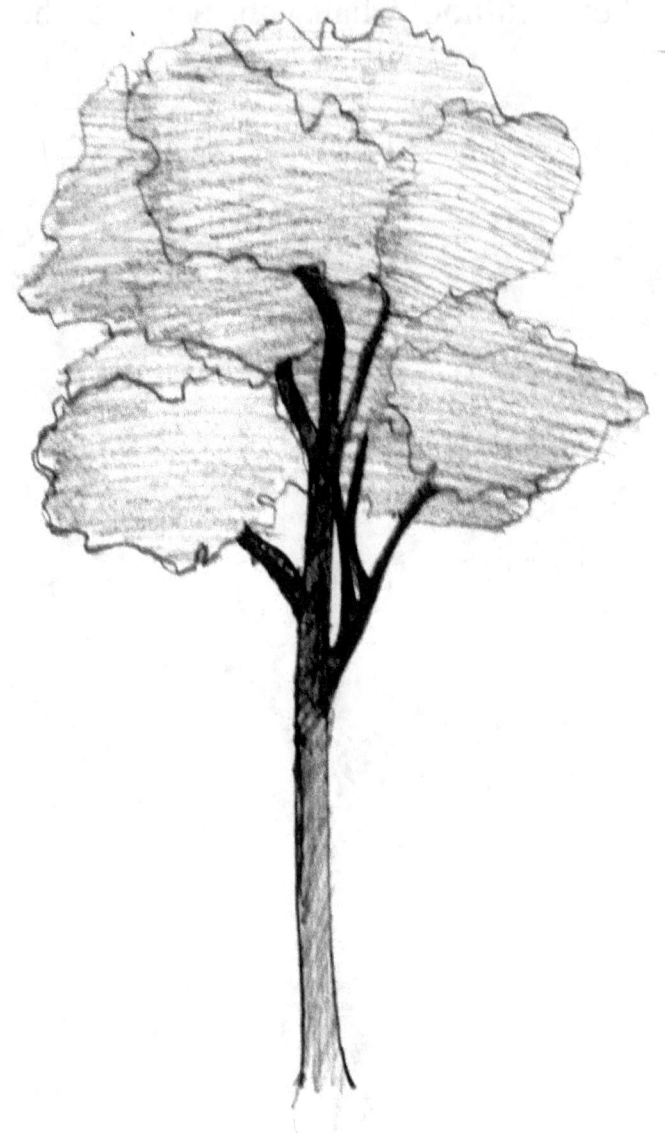

Based on the light source darken the appropriate areas of the trees leave and branches, and then once you've done that you get to start blending the lighter areas into the darker ones to achieve the look you see in the fifth and final step.

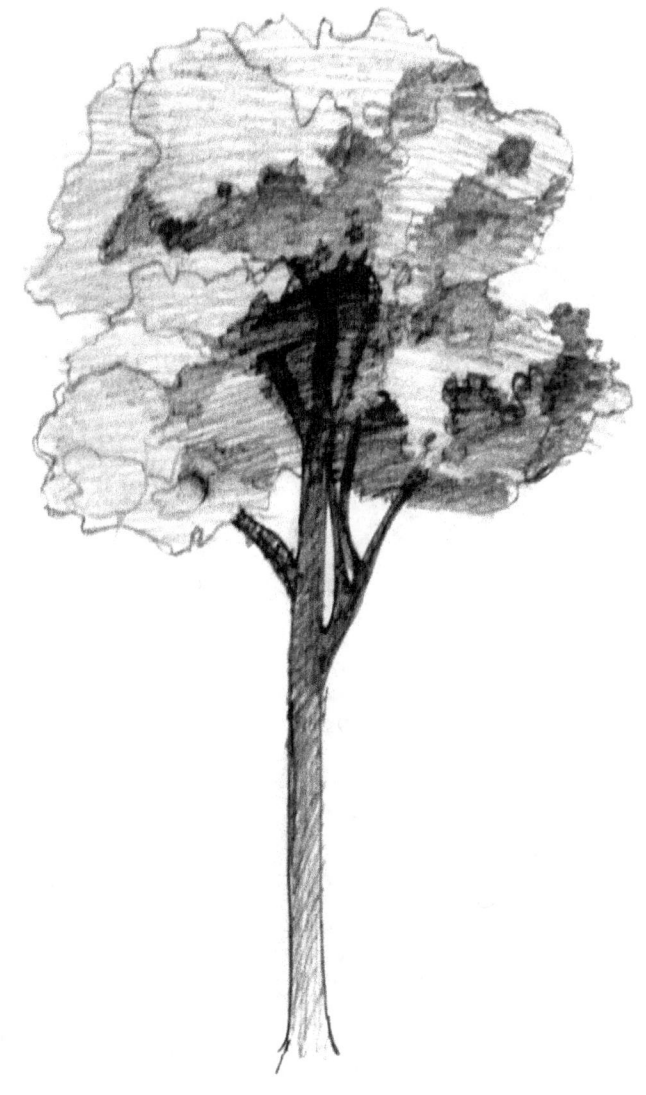

This image specifically is a very intriguing and fun one because it's simple and quick but it uses everything we've learned together, it's a great way to cap off this section and move on to something new and different that we haven't done yet.

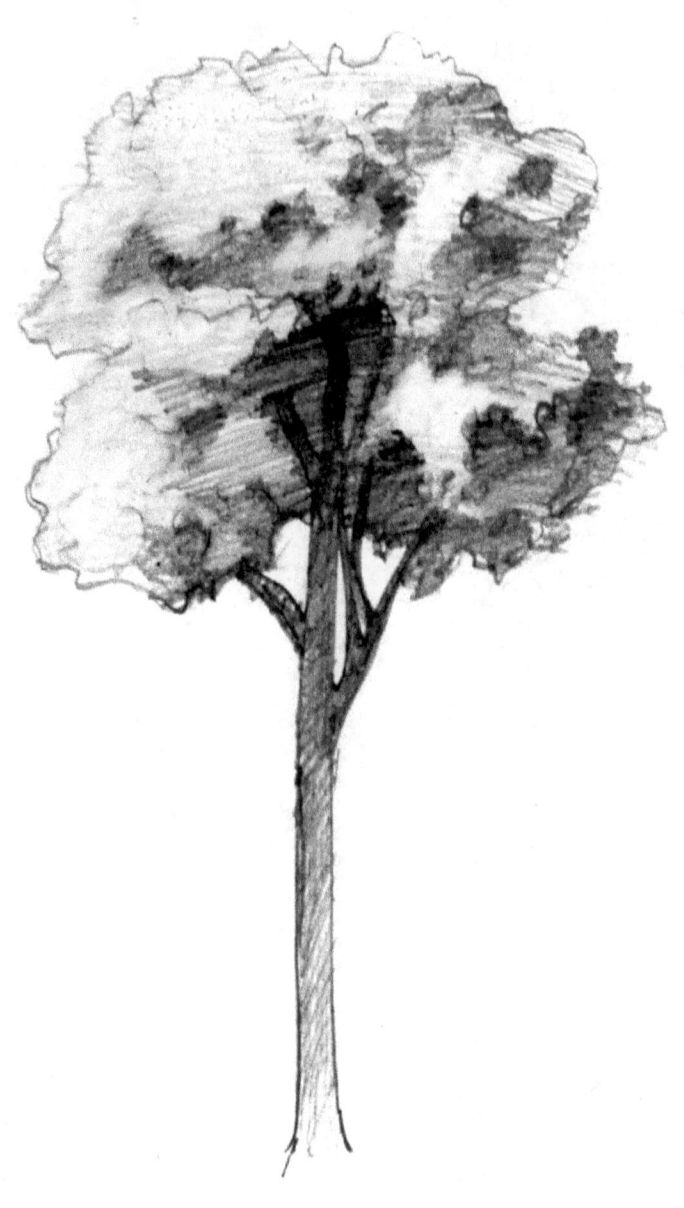

Animals

Picture 20. Dragonfly

This first drawing meshes two categories of nature, the animals and flowers. You have a dragonfly and a flower here. Start out with the small outline of the flower.

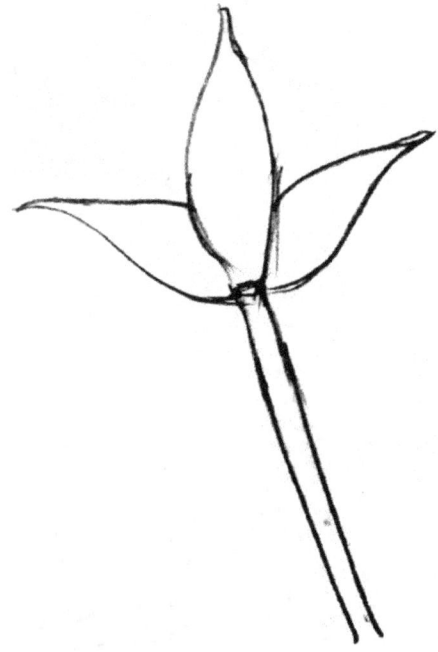

Then add in the petals using soft lining as you were taught (a). Then after that you can Sade in the stalk of the flower and then the petals. The shading here is fairly thick and dark. I recommend the hatch shading and make it dense. Once you have the petals and the entire flower shaded you start the dragonfly's outline (b).

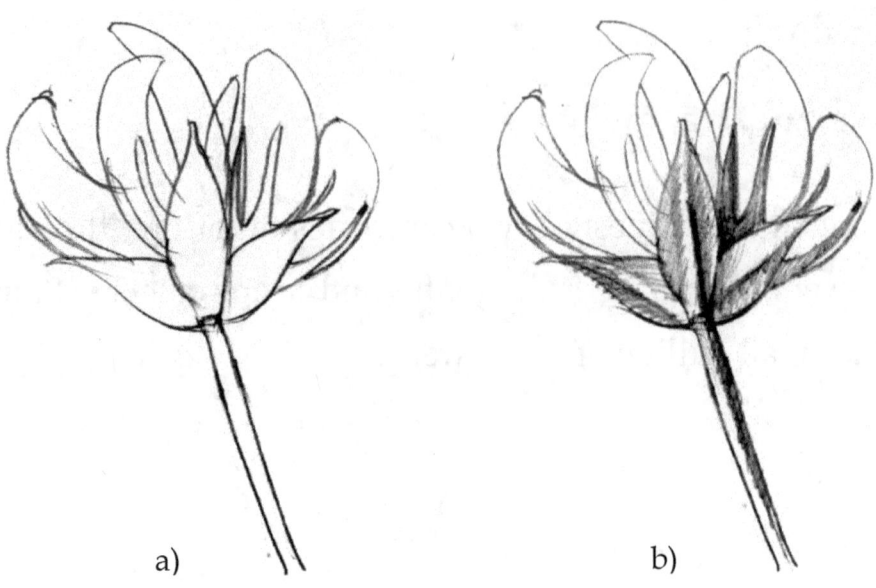

a) b)

As well if you looked close you'd see that the light source is coming from the left hand side.

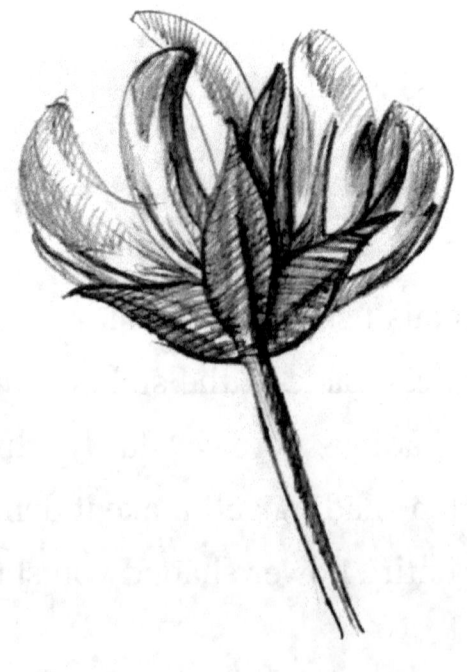

When you start the dragon fly use softer lining and then once you have the main body outlined using slightly firmer lines for the small details (c, d, e).

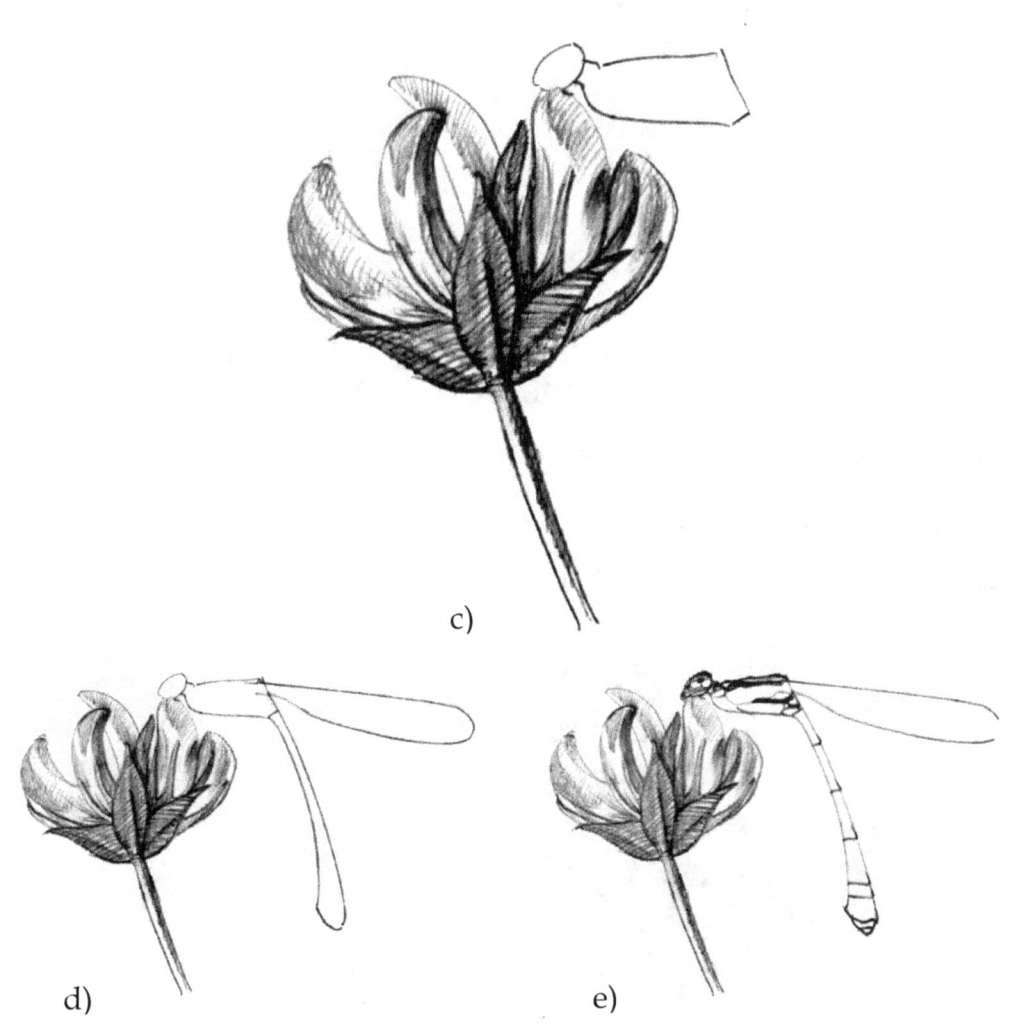

c)

d)   e)

Then you will want to start shading, again remember that with the light coming from the left hand side you will have darker shading on the right hand side.

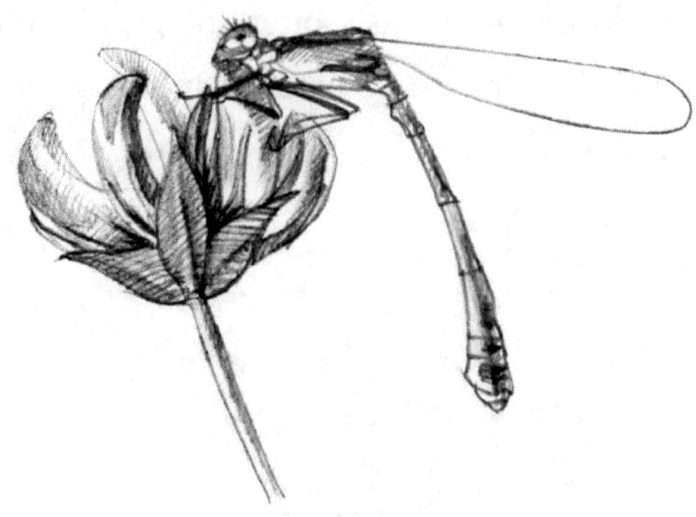

The dragonfly has very minute details but mostly its own the shading. The wings are the most complex so take your time with them and get the narrow lines with delicate precision.

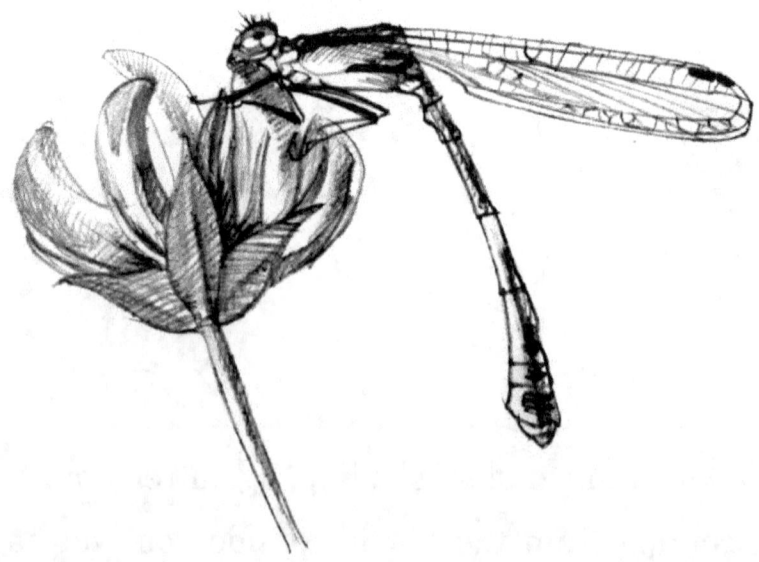

Once that's finished, you've completed your first drawing!

Picture 21. Snail

Time for the second drawing! This one starts out a little more simply than the last one. We have the first couple steps which consist of getting the outline of the snail made up (a). Start out with a slightly oblong circle and then add the snail body underneath (b).

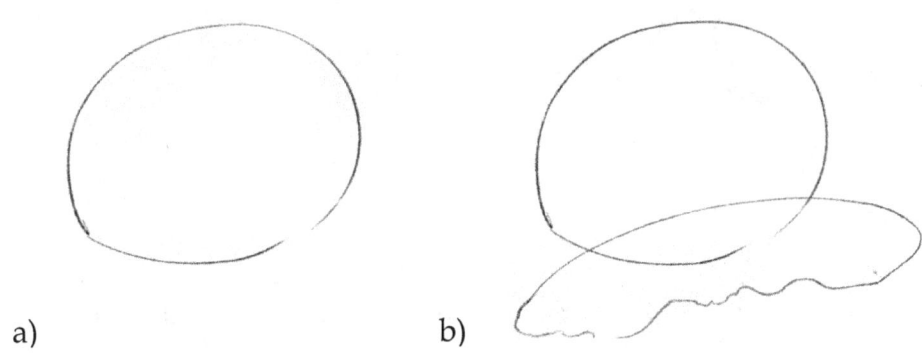

Next get the swirl in the shell started and start to fine tune and firm up the outline of the shell as you move along (e). The next step after that is to add in the antennae of the snail (d).

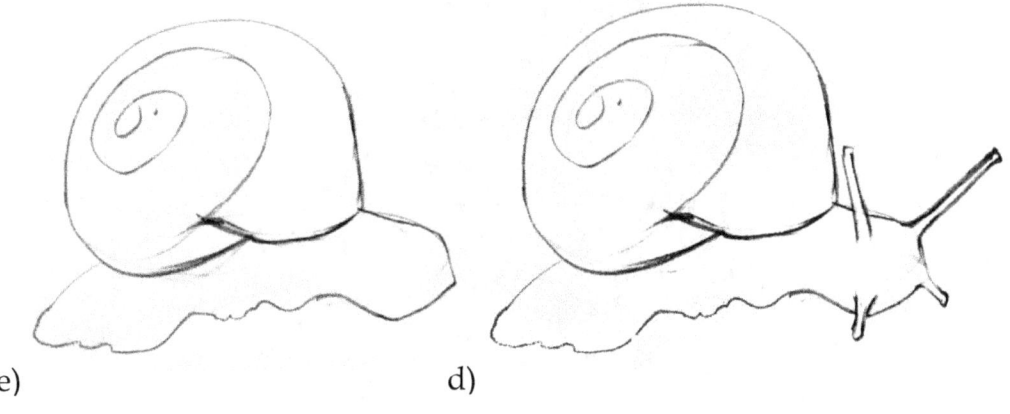

Once you have the basic and most simple form of the snail drawn you can start to shade it in (e). Start out by doing some back and forth basic shading along the shell. Darken it the most nearest the head of the snail (f).

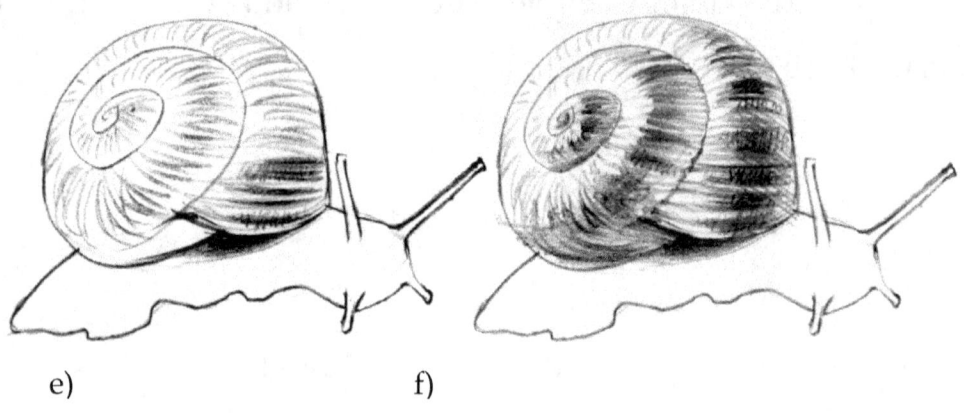

e) f)

Next up you'll want to proceed to use more back and forth darkening throughout the entire shell making sure to keep in mind that the light source is behind the snail and a distance away.

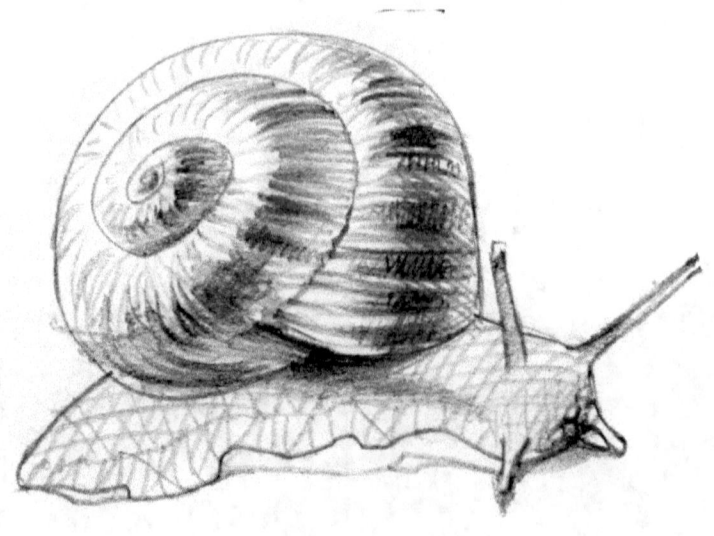

You can use the same light source plotting that you learned in the practice images you drew.

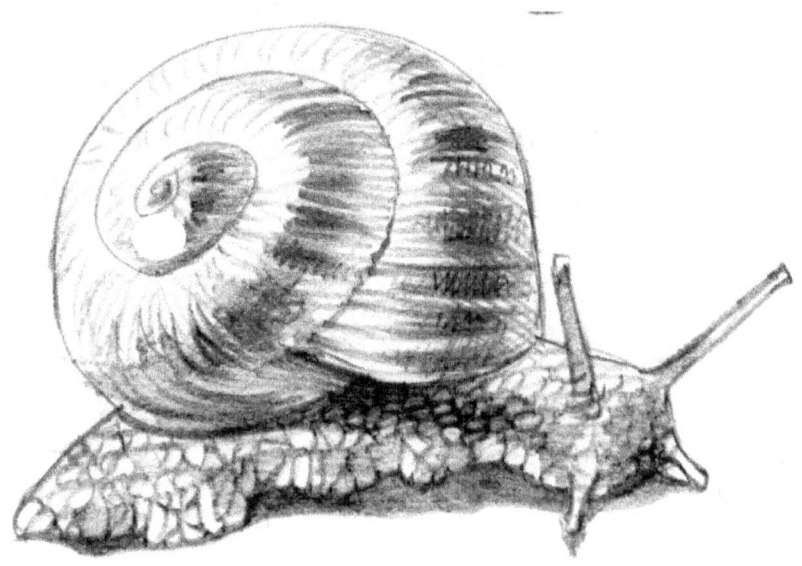

Them next you add the pattern to the snails body. You start out with simple line checkering to give the snail that texture. Those in the next step you get to shade in the body appropriately based on the light source. Also make sure to notice the falling shadow from the shell on the back of the snail.

Picture 22. Parrot

Let's keep this train rolling with the third image! This one is a parrot. It starts out with some simple fine line outlining akin to the last two. The difference here is that you are using longer lines and rounded edges (a). As well you need to take into account the layering of the parrot's feathers as you proceed forward (b).

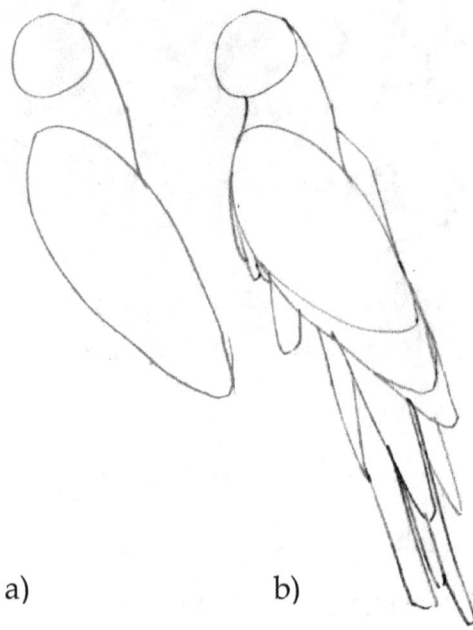

a)   b)

Then you get to the head and start to add the details in. You have the beak which is sharper and fine lined and then you have the bold lines of the cheek patterns and the small beady eyes as well to contrast. The shading starts on the head of the parrot and moves down to the wings.

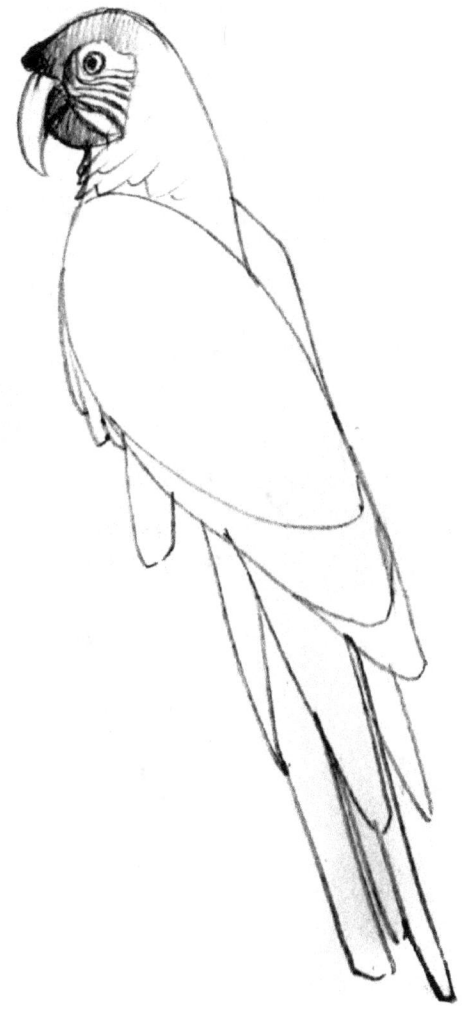

The shading nearest the beak is the darkest meaning you can assume that the light source must be behind the parrot.

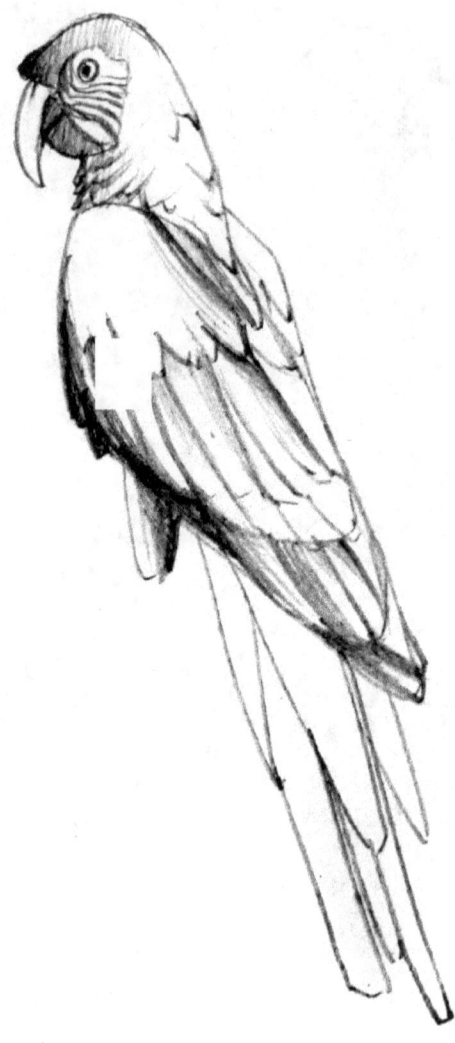

This is further confirmed as you start to shade in the wings lightly mostly using some light blending of the shades. This shows you that the only shadow on the feathers is mostly just from the layered feathers above themselves.

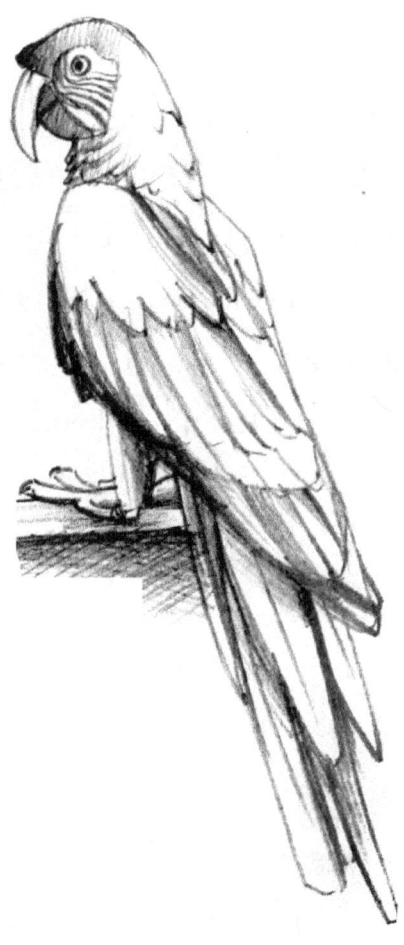

Then in the final step you draw the surface that the parrot is standing on and see that the shading is darkest underneath the bird dictating the light source perfectly. As well we have the feet here with the sharp nails as well. Also you can see that the underlining of the parrot is very thick and densely lined as well.

This is a simpler project in terms of shading but the finer details are definitely noticeable.

Picture 23. Penguin

Next we get to draw a personal favorite animal of mine, the penguin. Start out with a basic outline of the penguin's tummy, and then add in a spot for the tail and the head (a, b). Next up you'll want to outline the neck, head and beak (c). From there we begin shading in the image itself. You have the feet, the tail and the head where we color in the natural colours of the animal.

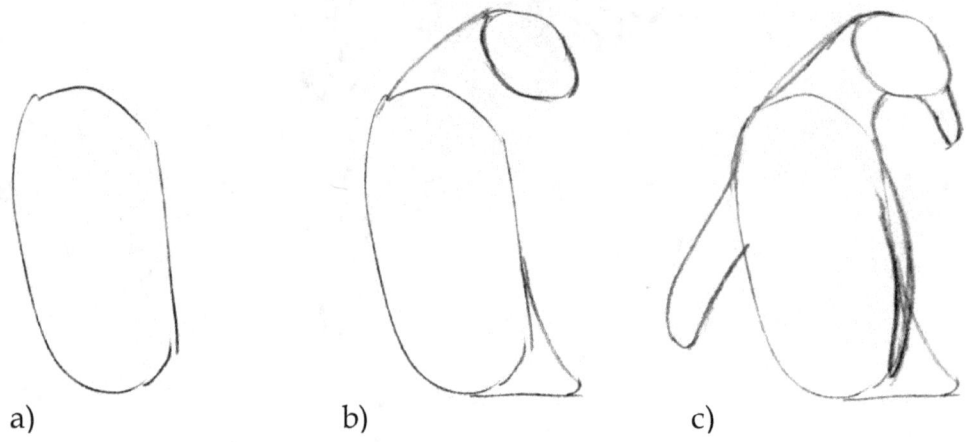

a)   b)   c)

Then once the colouring is done on those features we color in the neck and then the wings. That is the colouring finished and we have a basic penguin. The next step is to turn it from a basic penguin to a very artistically rendered penguin.

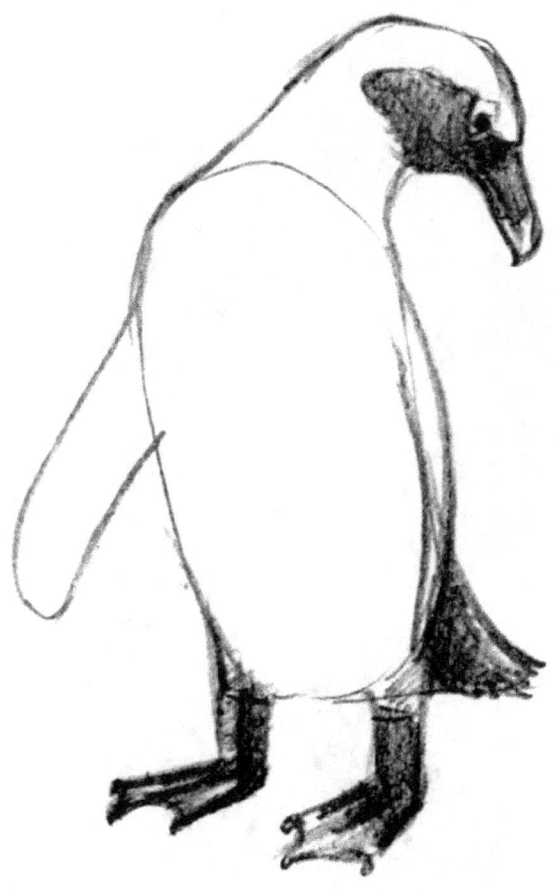

To do that you start out by figuring the light source is coming from the left hand side probably higher up and then plan accordingly.

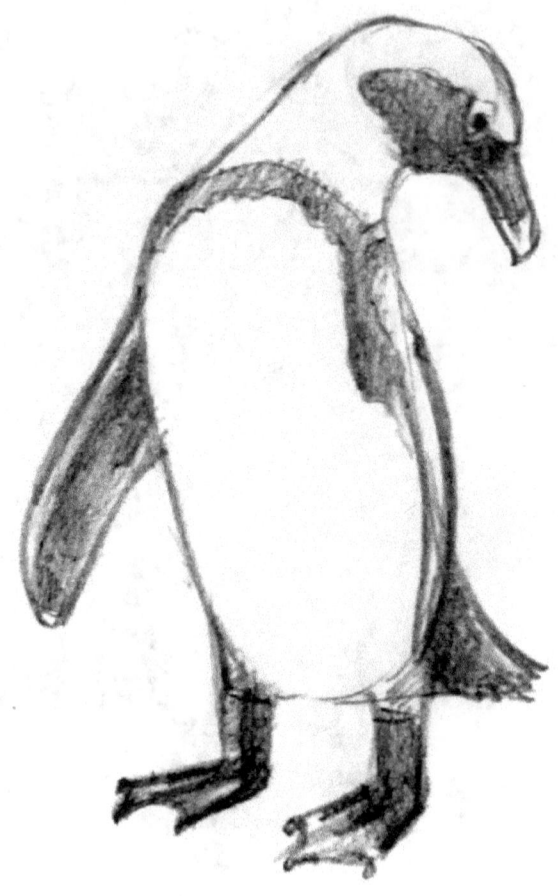

You will then notice that the shading is along the torso of the penguin and the underbelly and side.

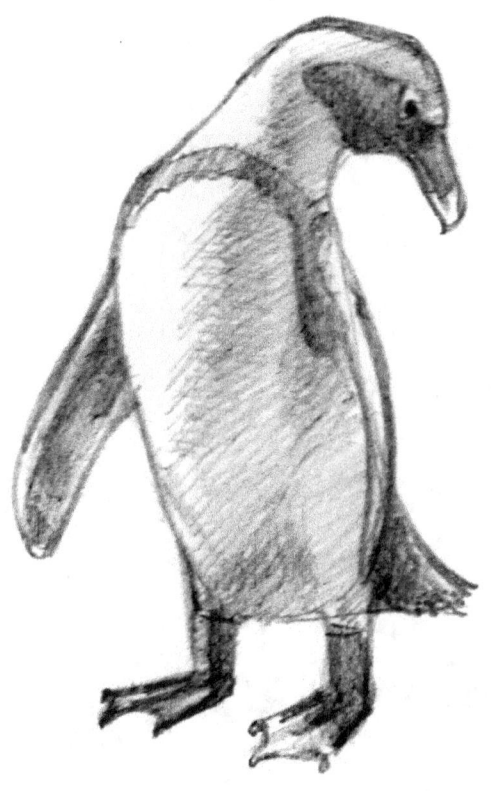

Here it's a simple cross hatch and it's not too thick or dense. It's a much softer form of shading and you can really utilize the blending along the top of the head and neck and stomach. To really highlight is the whiter portions of the penguins.

The final step is to do the falling shadow of the penguin which as you can see is much darker than the shading on the penguin itself. This is fairly simple if you follow the guidelines from the practice images and account for any distant shadow or enveloping light.

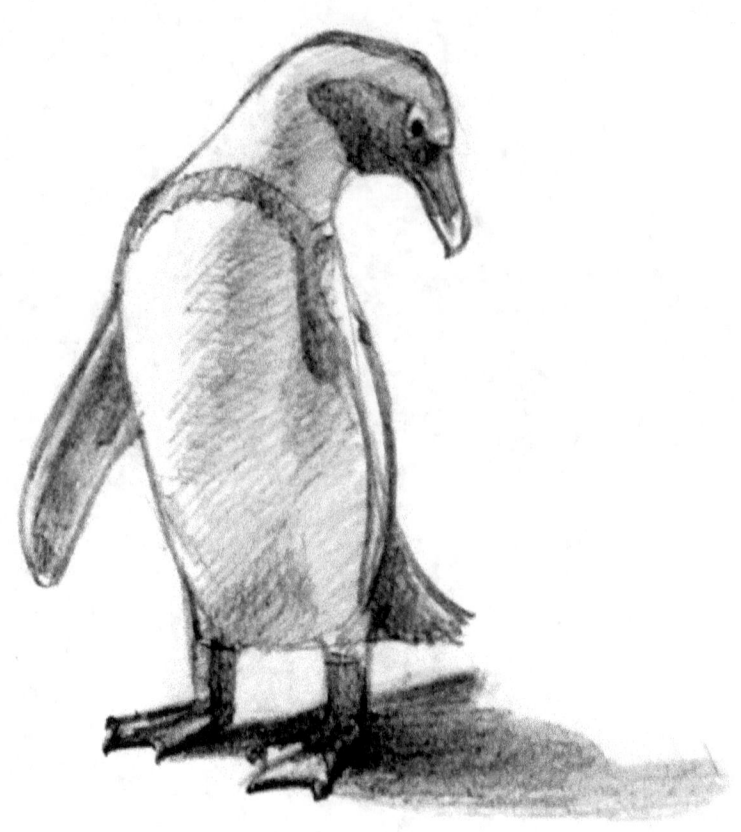

Picture 24. Crawfish

Now we have a very interesting creature to draw here. This is one of the first ones we are doing that has such an elaborate pattern on its back. As well as that it has some very fine detailing on it too.

Start out with the basic outlining as per usual and then once you get to the third step take a second to recalibrate your positioning. You will want to take it slow from here to make sure you get it all down right (a). So draw the whisker-like tendrils and then the eye (b). Then you start shading right away from there, very dark shading too.

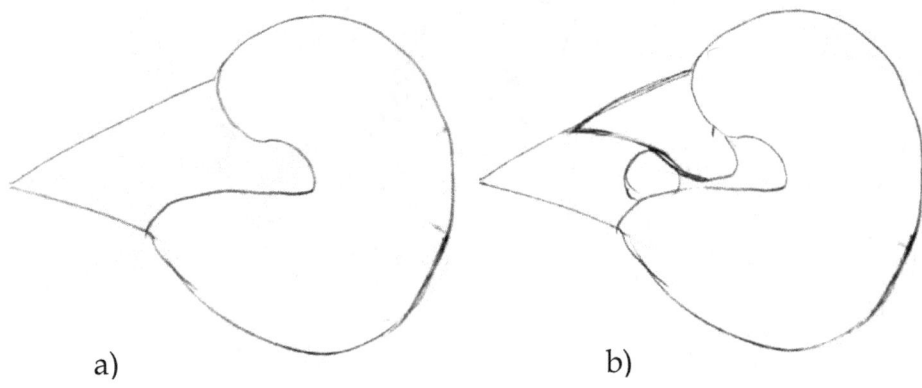

a)   b)

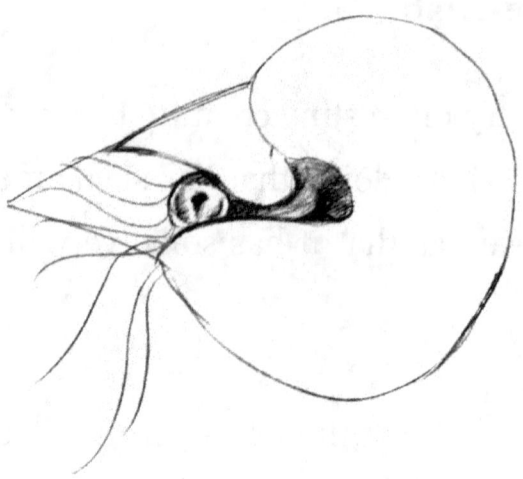

Next you need to outline the pattern on the shell and get a light cross hatch started on the head of the creature.

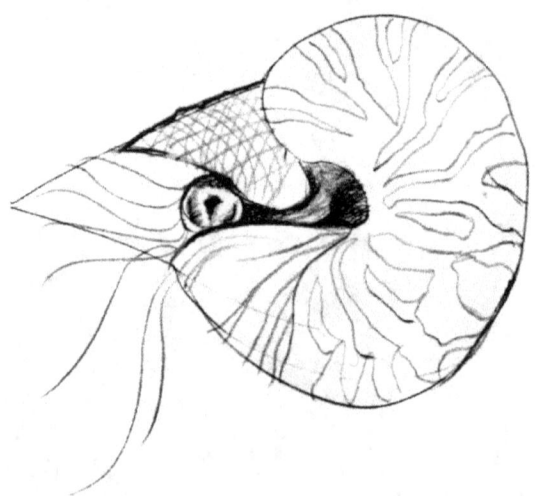

The next step gets elaborate suite quickly. We color in the outline on the shell and then shade in the top of the head with thicker and firmer patterning.

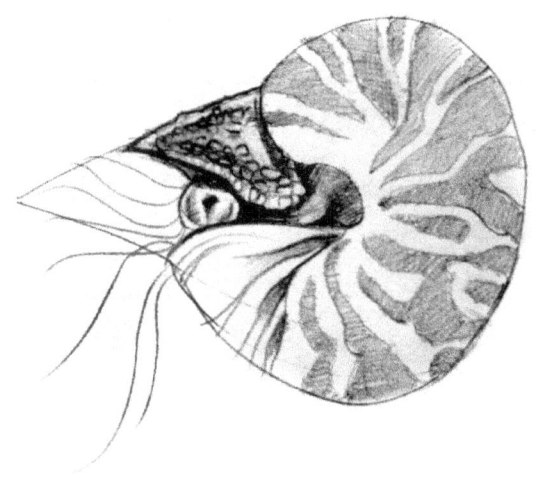

The next step is when we account for the light source. You can see that it must be from the far left. As well those tendrils we started on become much more layered and thought out here as well thicken them up with more lines and then shade underneath the layers as well.

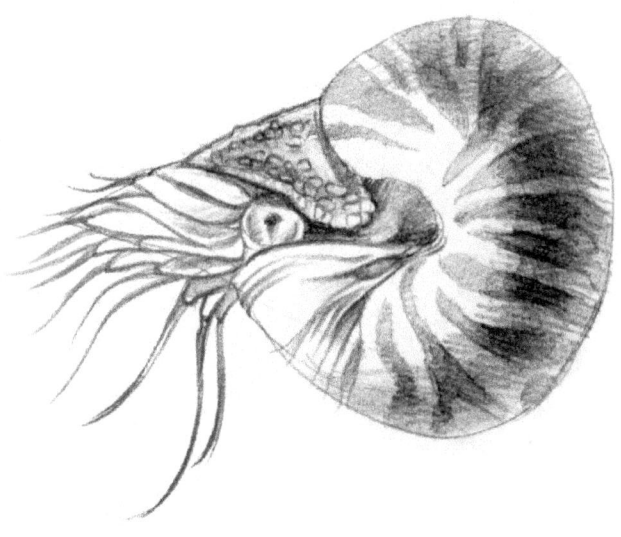

Finally you want to make sure that you shade the shell correctly in a rounded pattern accounting for broken shading and enveloping light as well.

Picture 25. Wallaby

This next image is a step down in complexities and focuses more on the intrigue of the animal itself. What we have is a baby kangaroo, or a wallaby. The basic outlining is the starting place.

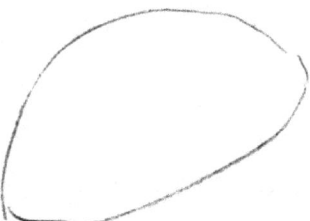

Once you have the basic body shape you add on the head and then the legs (a). Then we move on to the arms and then we start to get into the features of the head (b).

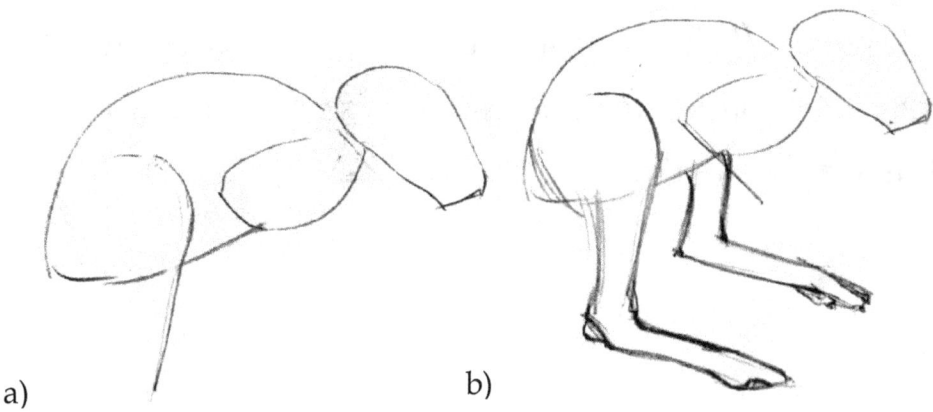

The ears and eyes are as well as the snout. Make sure to color the eyes in to begin with and then we can get into the shading (c, d).

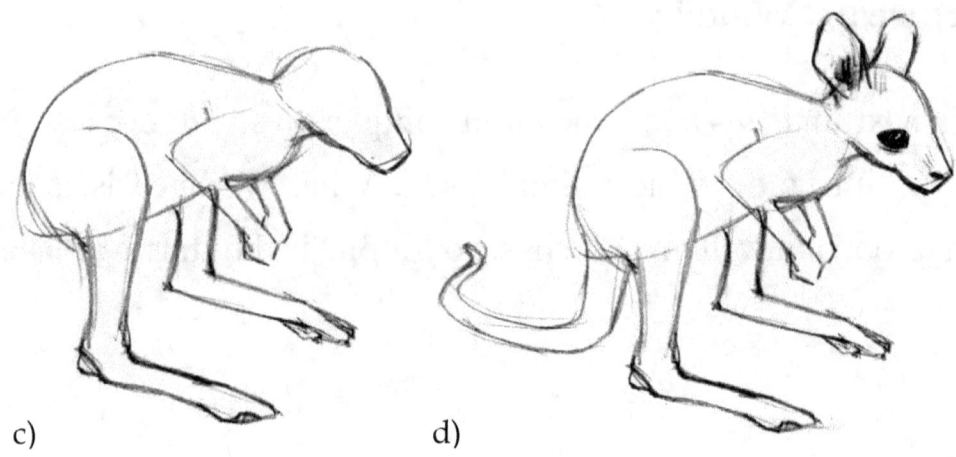

c) d)

Also make sure to notice that the tail was included in the last step, if you missed it because I didn't mention it right away then just make sure you are always double checking your work, you want to try and stay one step ahead.

Start out be shading around the edges of the outline, its darker shading but in thinner sections. The exception to start out is the animals hands which are shaded quite darkly, which can indicate that the light source must be somewhere that would leave the hands unexposed to the sunlight.

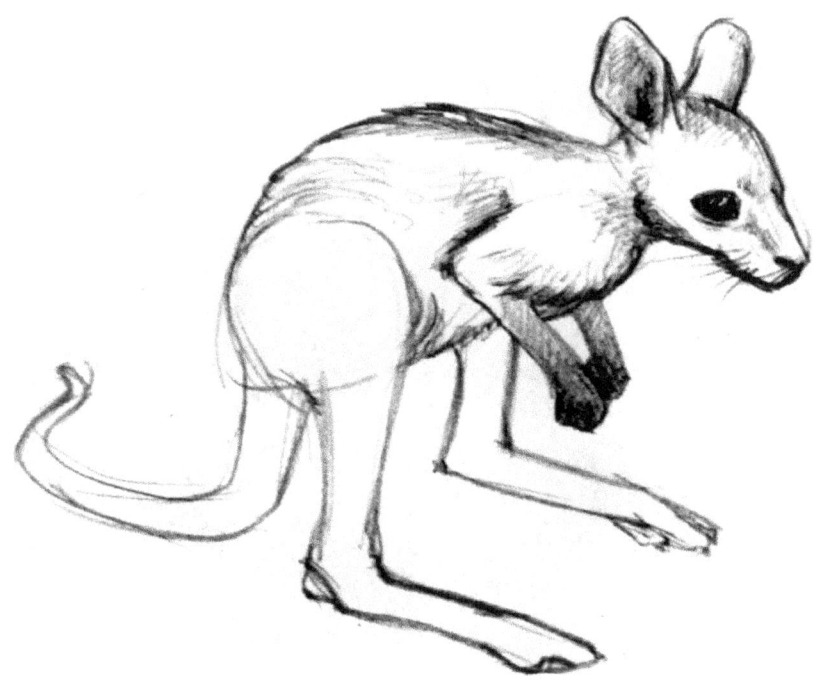

In the final step we finish up the shading of the tail and the legs, which both get a darker shading treatment much like the hands. As well we have the fallen shadow which stays mostly limited to underneath the animal directly. Which is also a tell tale sign of where the light source must be.

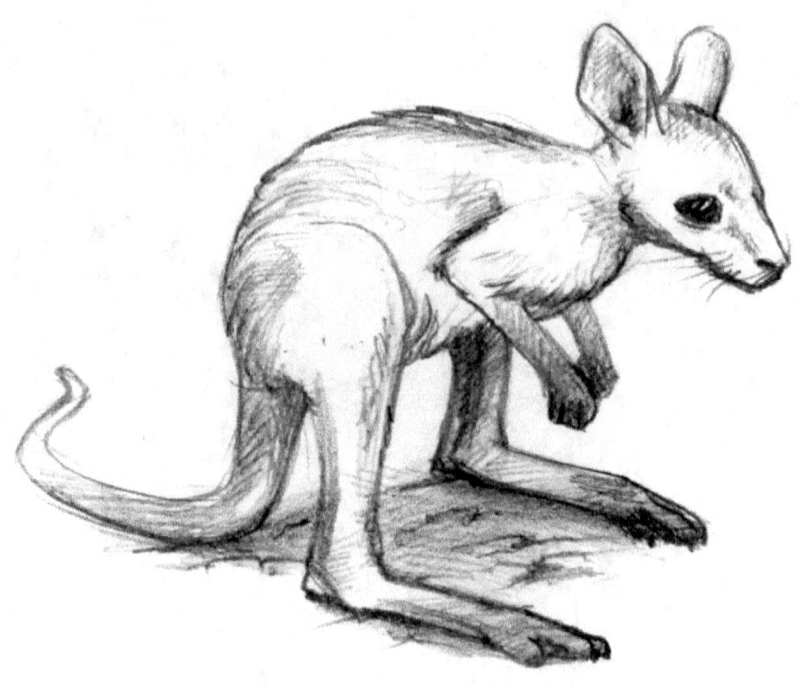

That means the image is finished! More simple but also effective and looks great, you don't always need to complicate the images you draw either, sometimes you'll want to for realism, but sometimes the best way to achieve the realism is to keep it simple.

Picture 26. Fish

To continue on it's a brief streak of simplicity. This next drawing is a little easier than some of the starting ones. This also marks the halfway point in this section! That means you are halfway to getting to draw some lovely flowers and trees!

Start on the outline, it's very round but not perfectly, and then from there you'll add what will become the head of the fish, and then you get to draw in the fins. These are very oblong in shape and don't require a ton of detail yet (a, b, c).

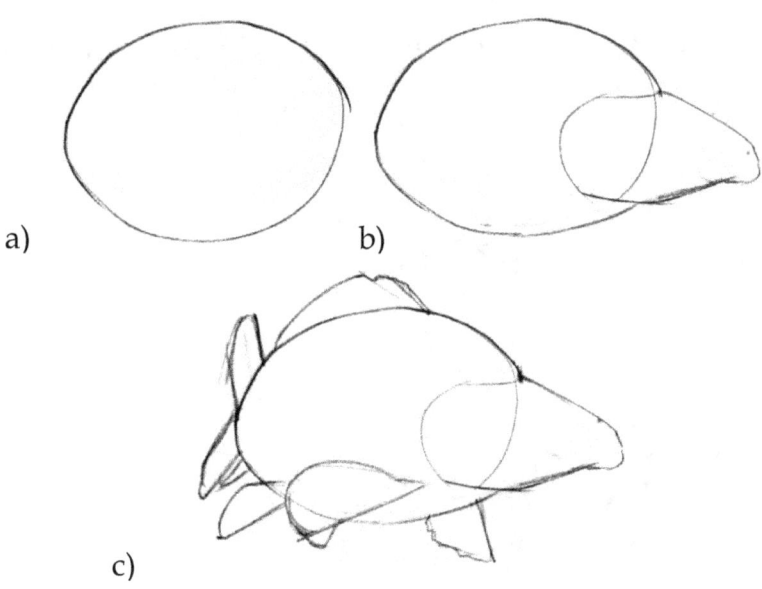

Once you have the head and the fins you get to start adding the important details. Start out by adding some patterned line work to the fins, and then the mouth and eye. As well the head gets its lining on it to dictate its fish look.

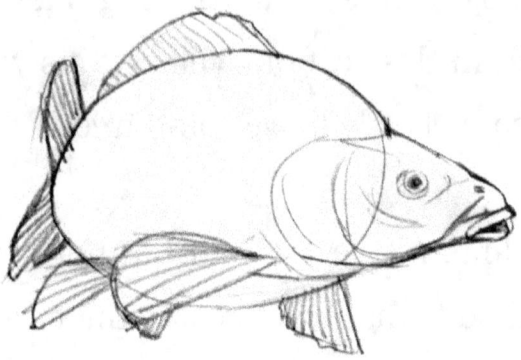

The next step we do a loose cross hatch on the body of the fish and also darken in the fins. This isn't the proper shading but it's the colouring of the fins, so darken in where it dictates in the image.

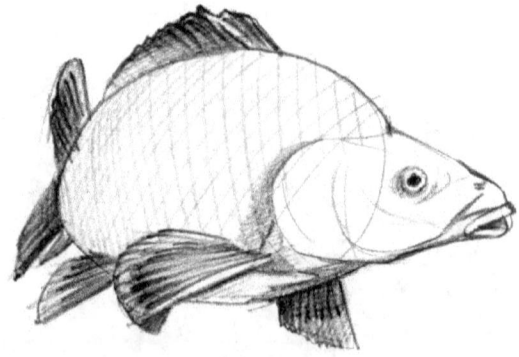

The final step is the shading, since the creature is likely in water we don't have any falling shadow to deal with this time. Instead we have the heavy shading along the scales and fins. Including the head of the fish and its gills are. This is a good example of broken shading because as you know when light hits water it's refracted and the light rays can be split up and shot in any which direction.

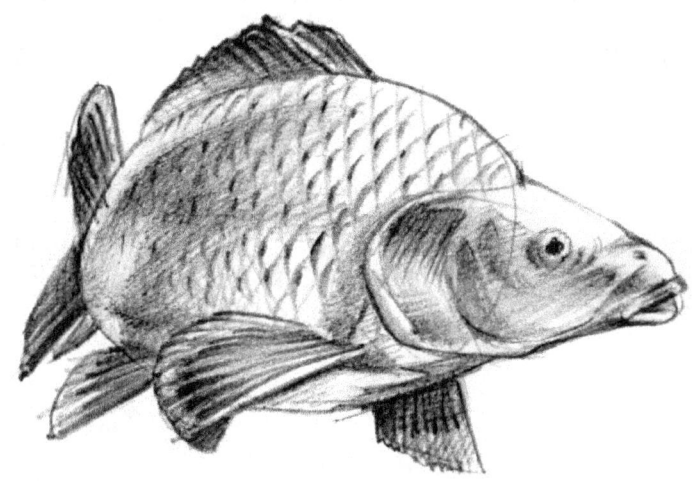

Mostly the end game is a very well detailed and shaded in fish, as you see in the final step up above.

Picture 27. Octopus

Let's get back into a slightly complicated drawing again. Here we have an octopus. The layering here and the shading is very complex and can be misinterpreted very easily. However you have had those practice images which means you should be able to follow along quite easily.

Start out with the basic outline as per usual (a). Create a very nice and uniformed foundation for the image and the shading that will ensue (b, c).

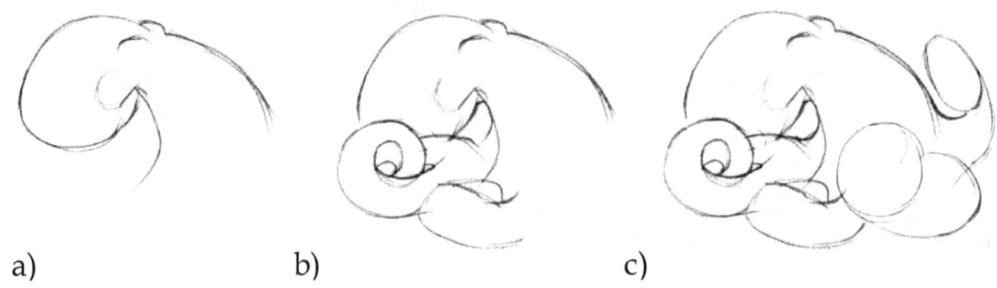

a)   b)   c)

Next you start shading right away at the back of the head of the octopus. You want to do some soft shading to begin and make sure to include the spikes that are on the head of the octopus. Also the eye is included there and you don't want to miss that.

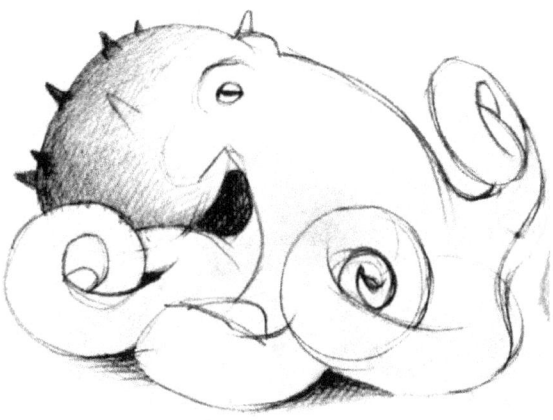

Then we throw you right into it and you need to shade each tentacle as shown. You can hazard that the light source is most likely coming at a low angle head onto the octopus. It is a safe bet and sometimes that is the best when you are dealing with a complicated subject like an octopus.

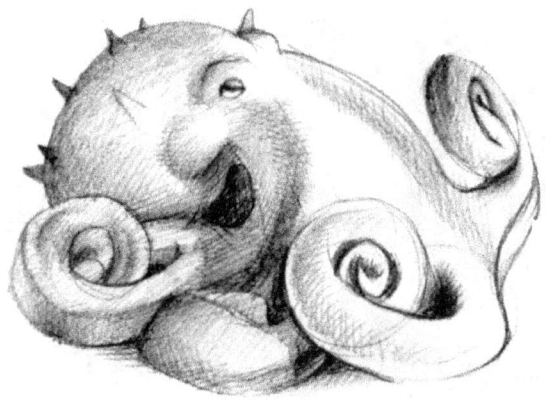

The next step after that is to get the suction pads on the bottom of the tentacles. You want to shade around each one individually as well to make sure you keep that level of realism in the drawing.

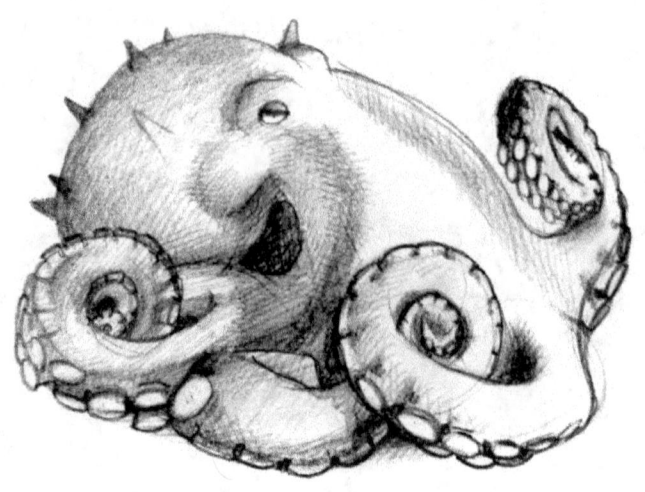

The final step you can see that you need to add more texture to the head of the octopus as well as include darker shading at the back of the head. This is fairly easily done by utilizing the texture and blending techniques taught a few chapters back.

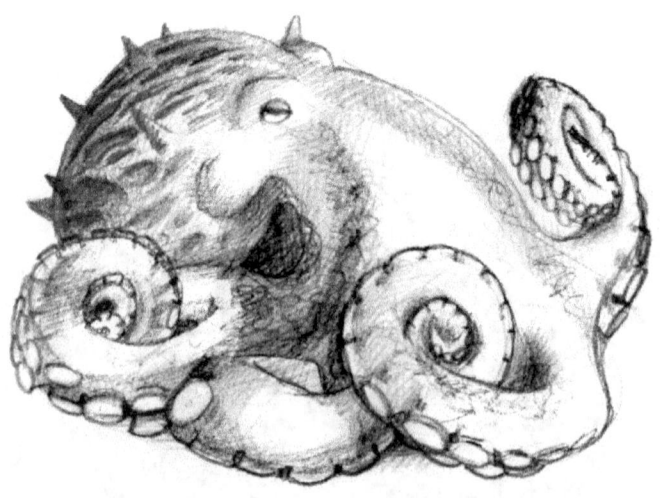

Picture 28. Dog

The actual drawing of this animal isn't difficult but the shading can be considered as elaborate if you factor in the muscular body of the dog as well as the multiple limbs in the image.

Start out with the outlining and the legs (a). Progress from there and do the outline of the head and then the ears. Then once you have that start sketching in the eyes and the snout. You can also see some detail on the mouth here too (b).

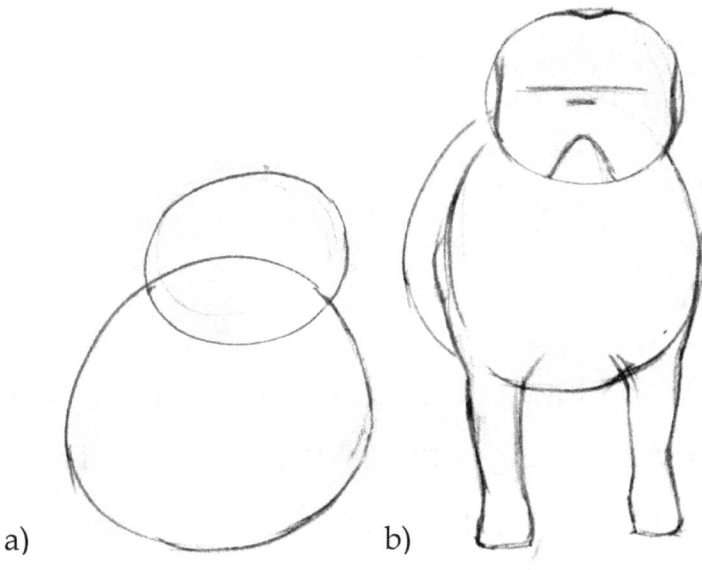

Once you have those details ironed out its time to get straight into the shading. Here the light source is something of a mystery but if you look at the final step and see where the fallen shadow lies you can start to infer that the light source must be almost directly above the dog but slightly offside to the back a bit.

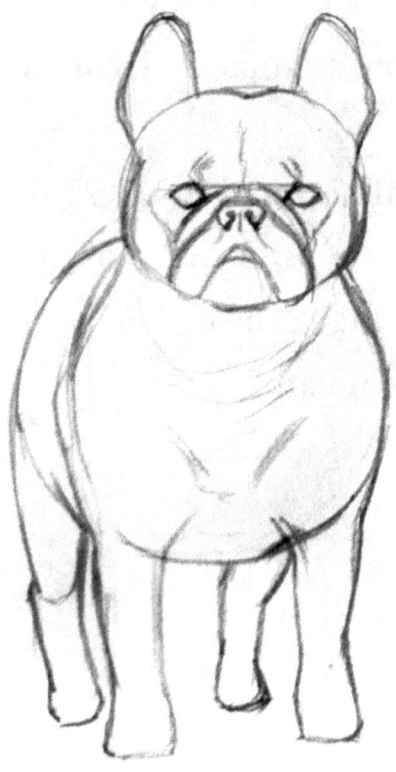

With that detail in mind you are able to fine tune your shading to match what you are doing with the shading of the limbs and the body. The lower half of the face is very dark, especially around the eyes and the mouth. Them underneath the neck you have some dark shading, also around where the dog's muscles would be.

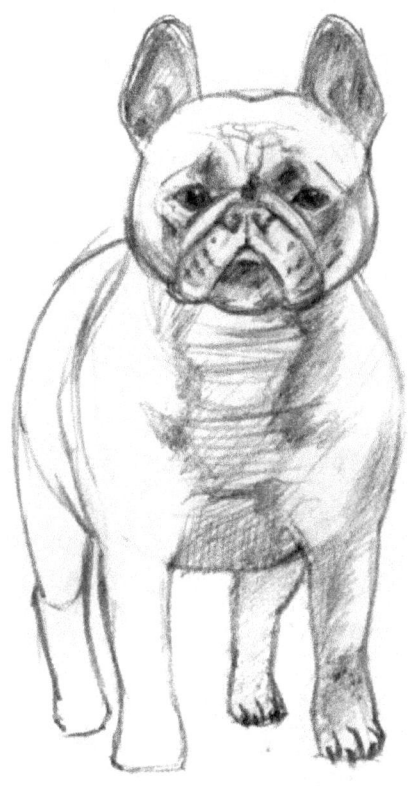

It is also important to note that the dogs back right leg is very well shaded on the inside, which is another good clue as to how two shade the rest of the animal.

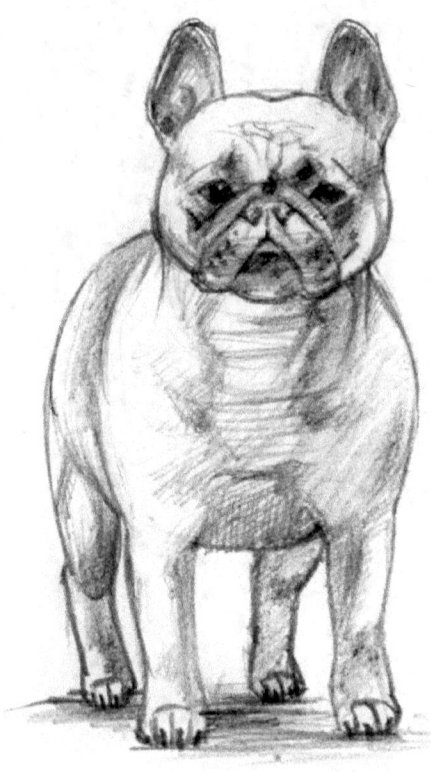

The key here with an animal that is front facing like this is to look for the areas that give away the secrets, like the back leg and also the snout.

Picture 29. Lion and Cub

This next drawing is important more for the fundamental layout of the image. As well it is a very touching and beautiful image that looks great when drawn nicely and shaded well.

Start with the line work of the lion (a). In this image we aren't drawing the entire lion but we are doing around half (b). We are however drawing the entire cub, despite the fact that the cub is half covered by the pay and arm of the lion (c).

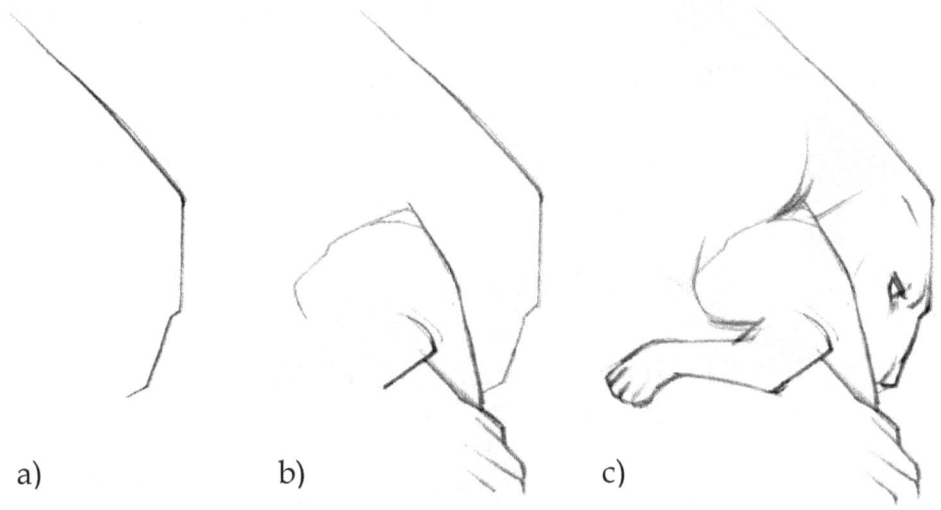

a) b) c)

Once you've gotten the lining done on both the lion and the cub you get started right away on the shading. We start with the cubs head and then we move down and shade in its body and its arms. Including the arm of the lion are.

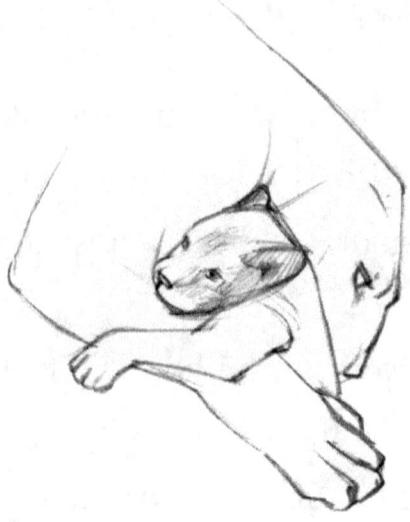

From there you can see that we shade the lions arm and also go back to do some light shading on the lions body, mostly outlining its muscles and features like ears and snout.

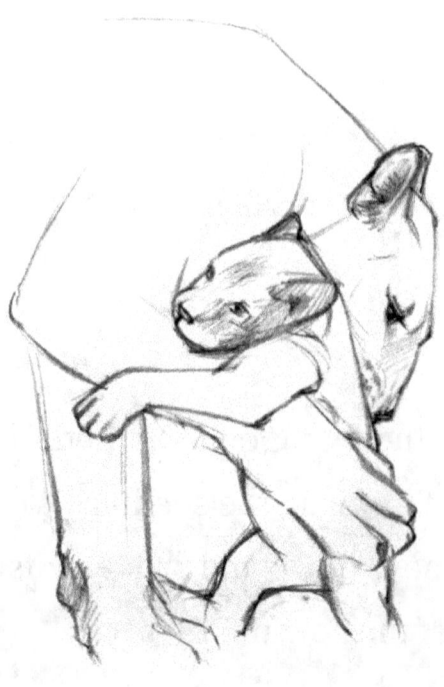

The truly special thing about this image is it's the first one we have encountered so far where we are actually adding in some of the nature from the world into the image.

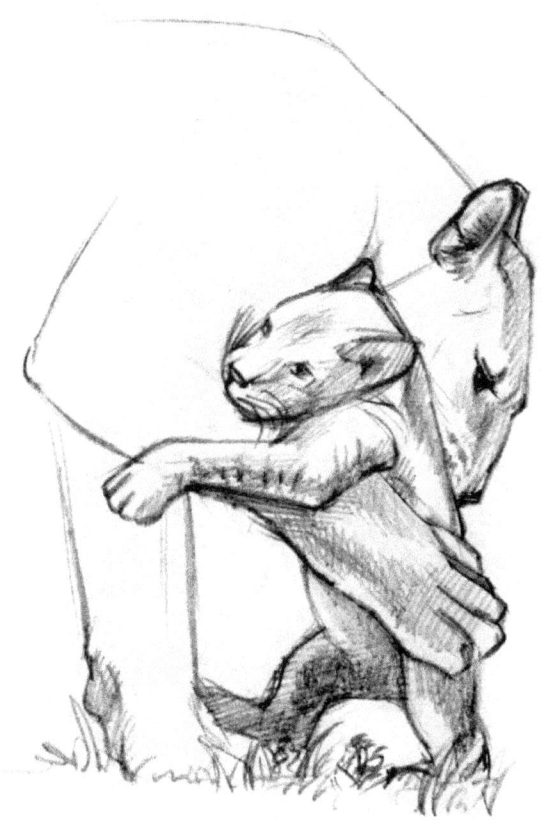

The grass isn't overtly detailed however it does add texture to the image. It makes it look very real and adds a nice flavor that can really make the difference between a drawing and a piece of art.

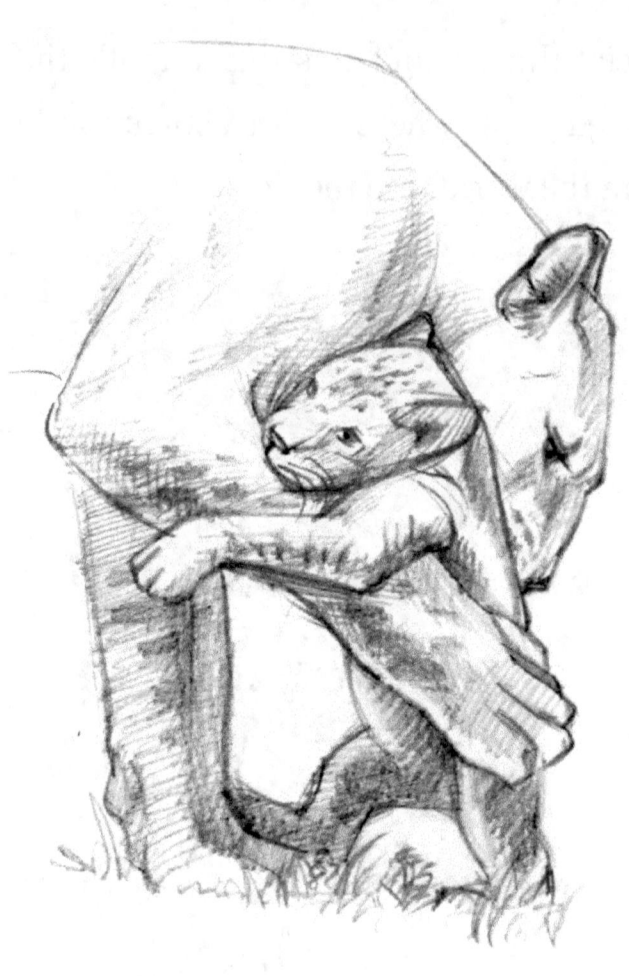

Picture 30. Fox

This image is an interesting one because there isn't a lot to the outline or otherwise the line work at all, however the detail is all on the shading.

Start out by drawing the circle that will become the main body of the fox (a). Then start drawing in the features and shaping of the fox's limbs and tail (b, c).

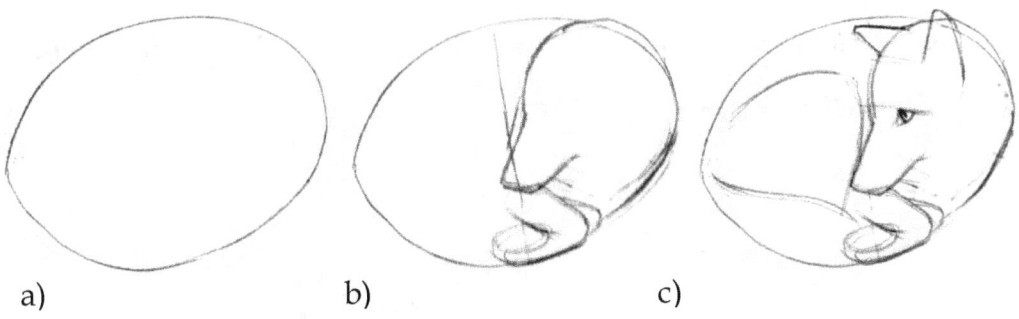

a) b) c)

By the fourth step you have all of the necessary imagery of the fox done and complete, and then its features need to be added in. Such as there are the ears and the eyes and the snout. All important features and really the only ones that need to be added that aren't primarily shading.

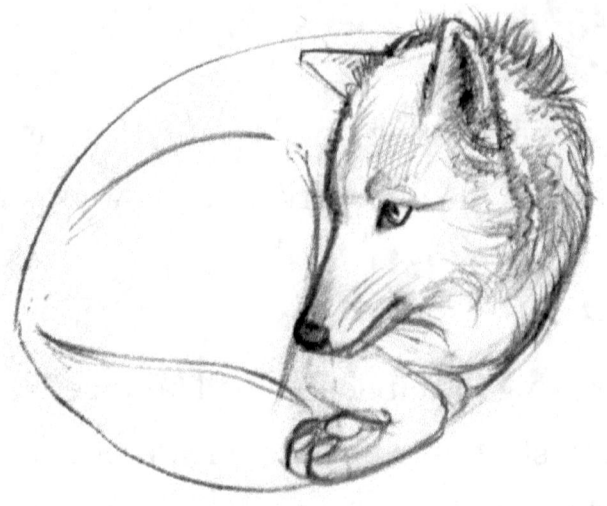

Next up you will want to shade in the animals fur. You can see that this is a very detailed and complex looking feat, however is fairly simple in execution.

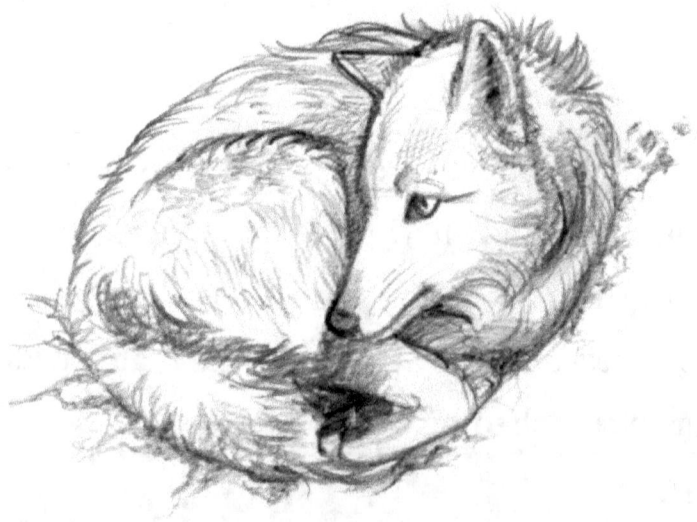

You will want to use small and individual sections of hatching to get the fur that patchy detailed look. As well you can tell that the

fox must be nestled into something, either the dirt or the snow, but with the way the detailing is done I would assume its snow.

Keep that in mind as you shade in the outline of the fox and make sure your choice of its resting place is reflected in the drawing.

This image is a good example of needing to decide on the animal's environment prior to putting pencil to paper. Nothing wrong with changing your mind but if the shading is reflective of the environment you want to decide ahead of time.

Picture 31. Antelope

Finally we are back to another one of the more simple drawings. Here we have something that is very certainly focused on the shape of the animal and selects a few details to highlight.

For instance in a quick overview you can decide that the horns and the tail are the most prominent features of the drawing.

With that in mind you can progress forward and know where to highlight the most. In order to start you will draw that strange first shape which you will essentially whittle away to get the actual body of the animal (a, b). Once you've done that you add in the horns and the legs (c).

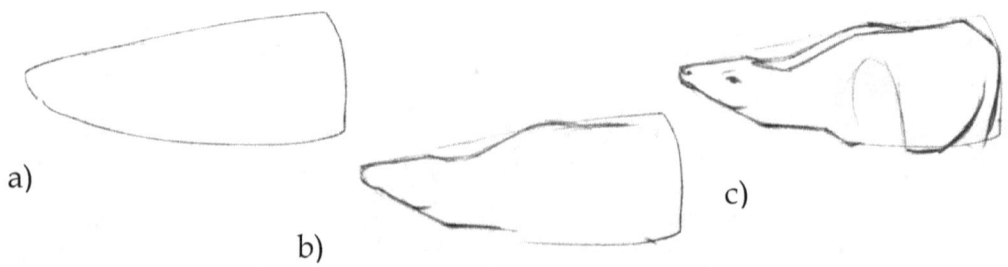

Compare that with the starting shape and you can see why you started that way and how it lent an important asset to the process (d). Then once you have the body and the horns you can color in the horns and then add in the tail (e).

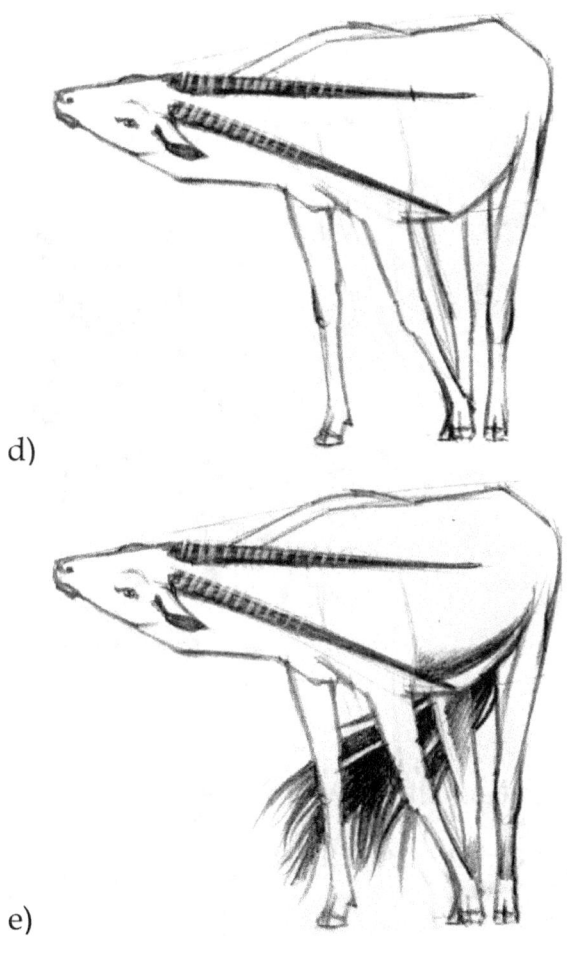

d)

e)

The tail is a massive amount of detail but luckily it is also mostly just black in design and is comprised of many lines. It is also easy to detail because it is impossible to discern the black lines from one another.

Finally you will be on the last step where you will shade in mostly just the haunches and the places where the body shapes change for joints or humps or muscles. As well the design on the head of the creature is colored in and the legs are shaded too.

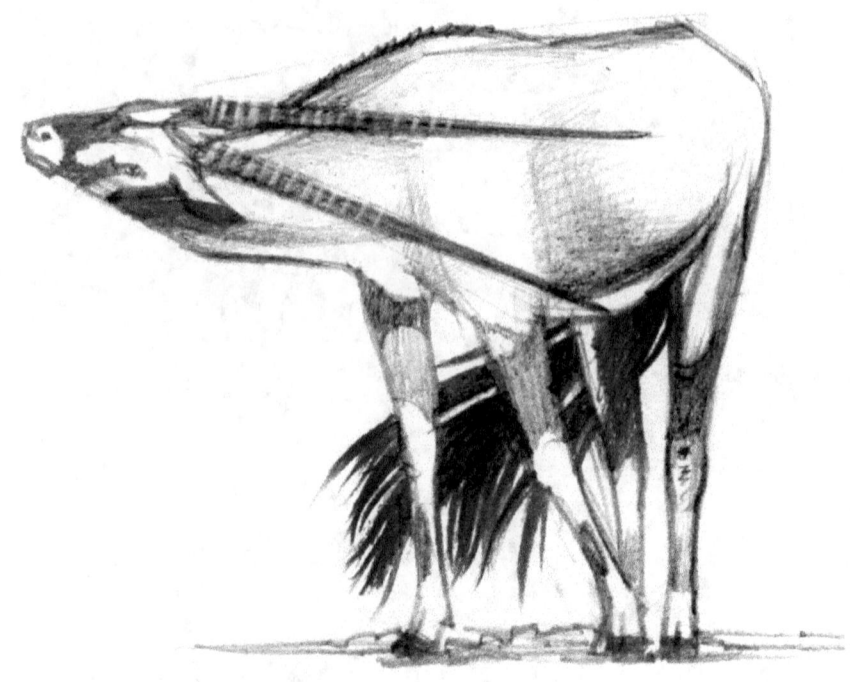

Don't forget about the shadow on the ground of the animal as well, an important detail for realism.

Picture 32. Vulture

This is the second to last creature and what you are looking at is a prehistoric vulture. It has a more scientific name but for artistic sake let's just focus on the drawing.

This one starts out simply requiring just outlining (a). Then around step three you can see that we start shading in the small wings and the little tuft of a tail (b, c).

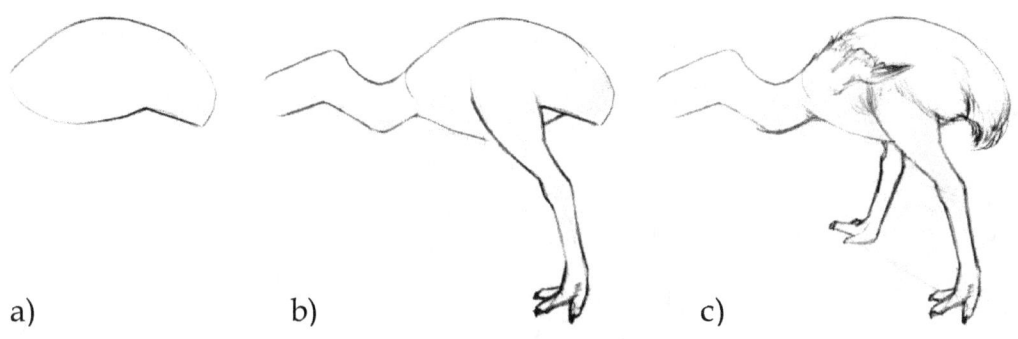

a)   b)   c)

The form there we pencil in the sharp beak, the tongue and the feathers around the face (d). That is an important part because the next step sees the shading of those areas almost right away. The neck is shaded and in such a way that highlights the muscle in the neck (e).

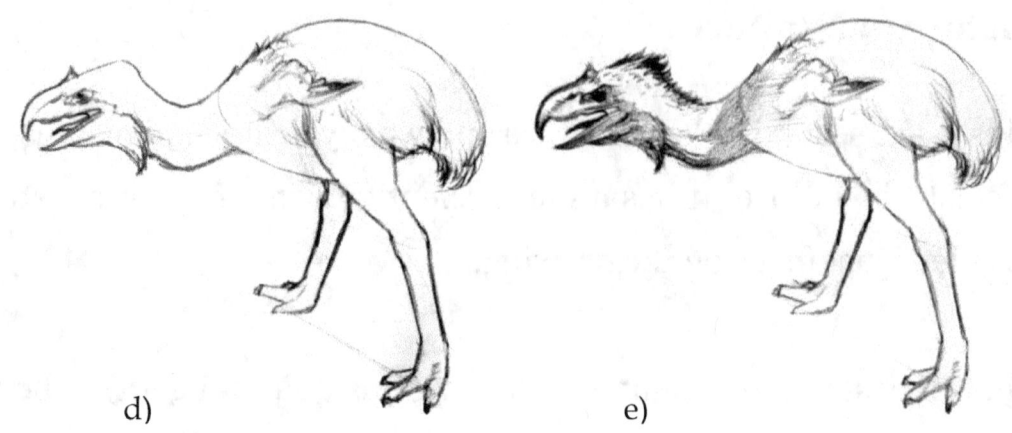

d)   e)

The step after that sees the feathers around the legs and mid section get colored in too. The leg furthest from the front of the drawing is shaded in very dark, showing that the light source is likely coming from where we are in terms of looking at the image.

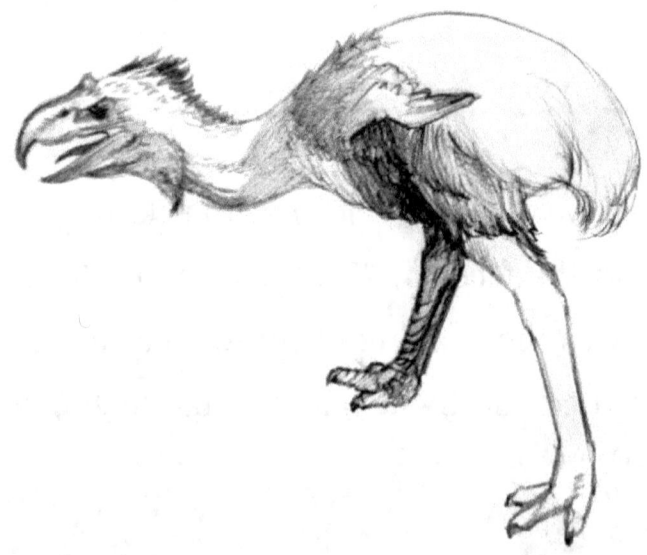

The feathers from there are completely shaded in and textured with some cross hatching and back and forth.

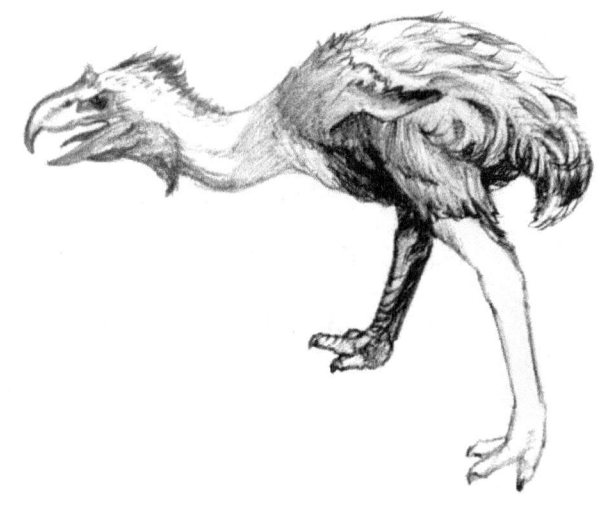

Them we add some features to the ground such as broken earth and some small sprouts of grass and foliage. This adds to the prehistoric theme.

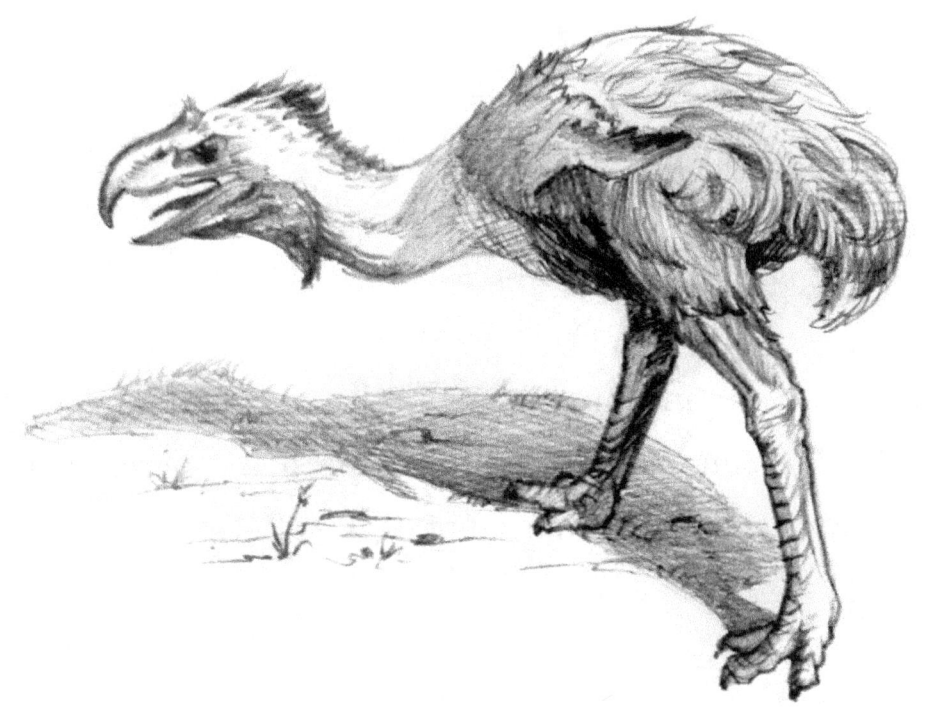

Picture 33. Stegosaurus

We have reached the final and last drawing in the animals section of this book. So far you have drawn all kinds of creatures and should be delighted to see that we have reached all the way back and brought a dinosaur as the final drawing in this section. How fun!

Let's start the same as usual with the outlining and the frame work (a). The once you've gotten the basic body shape, you get to start adding the plates that stick out of the back (b). You can see that there wind up being several rows of them as well as the spikes on the tail to add, draw legs (c).

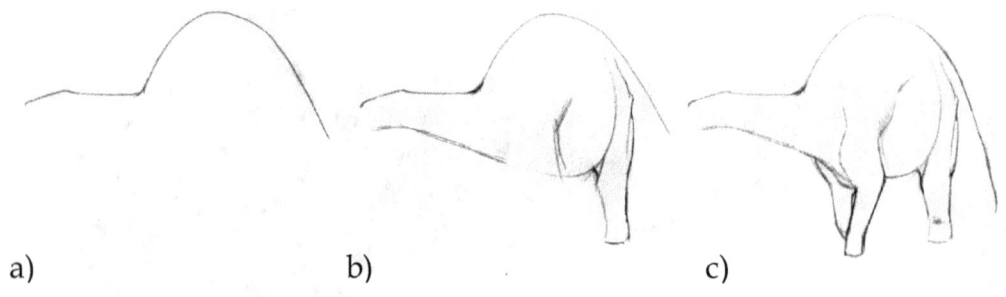

a)   b)   c)

From there you can start shading in the body naturally from the back to the front keeping in mind the light source, which is apparently coming from in front of it (d, e).

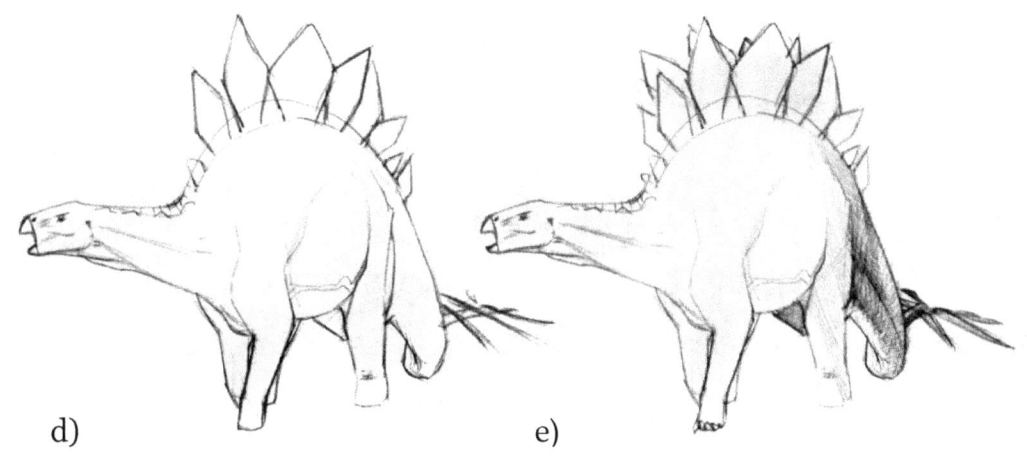

d)   e)

Then once that is taken care of you get to blend in a pattern to the body of the dinosaur (f). It is somewhat patchy but mostly staggered in a way that looks nice. Keep that in mind when shading in the plates and the falling shadow as well (g).

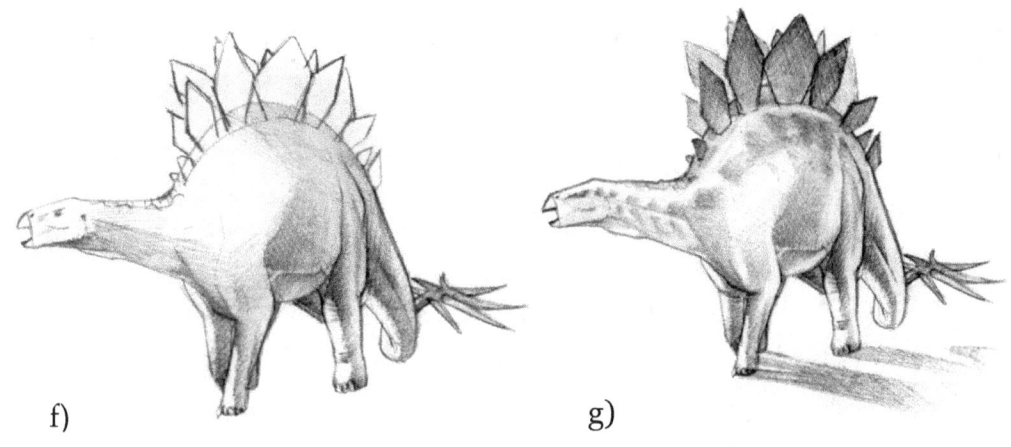

f)   g)

Take pride in your final drawing in this section and get ready to head over to the next section which is the Landscapes section!

Landscapes

Picture 34. City Streets

The first entry in the landscapes section is a truly detailed and complex looking image. The best instruction I can give is to follow those first three steps religiously. Use a ruler and add each one of those lines in exactly as it's laid out.

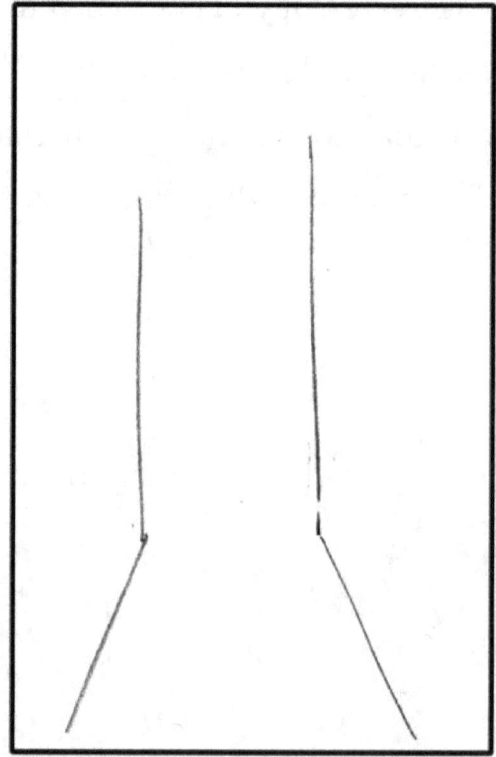

Then in the second step you can start adding in the design and interesting sections of the image.

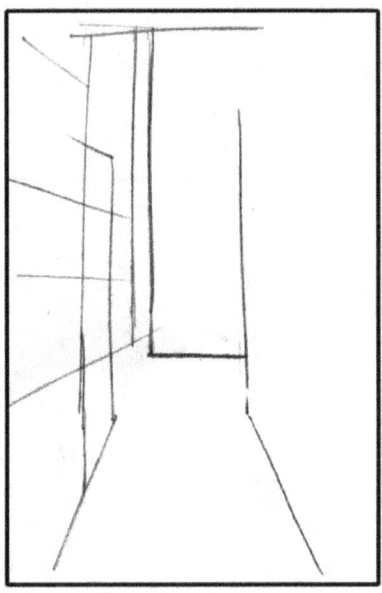

By the third step the setting looks nothing like it did in the beginning, to get that you need to be comfortable with going over the work multiple times with a pencil and eraser.

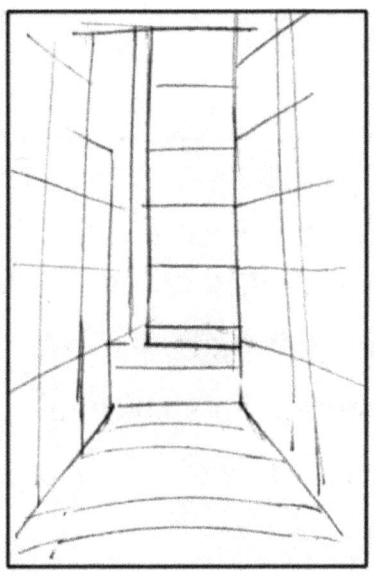

As well the details are all fairly minute here, really being created with the very tip of the pencil, then shading in is done after that.

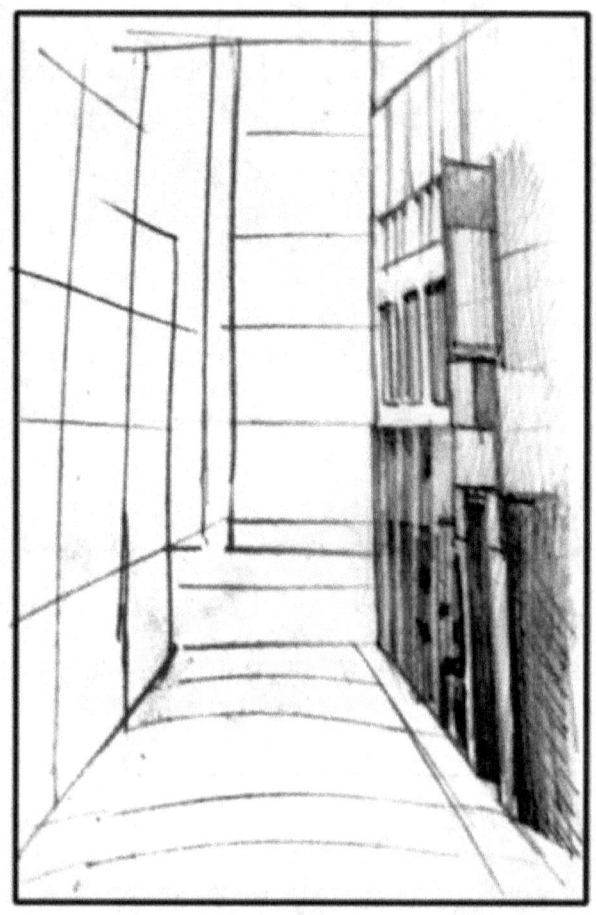

The last three steps focus on shading almost exclusively. This is daunting at first if you just look at it before you start, but once you've drawn in the store fronts and building faces and window ledges and street details you will have no problem adding in the texture and shading (a, b).

a)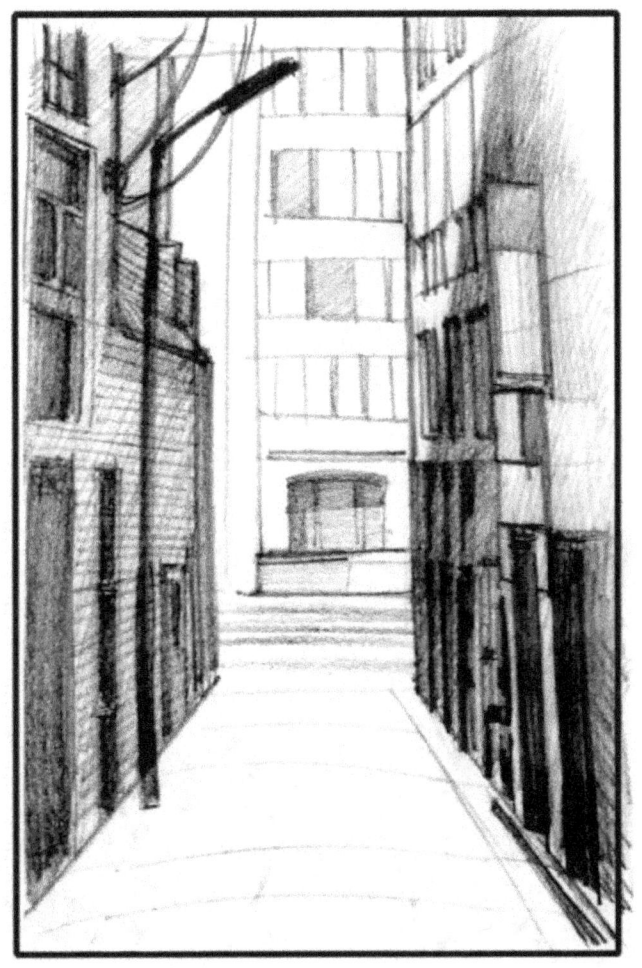

b)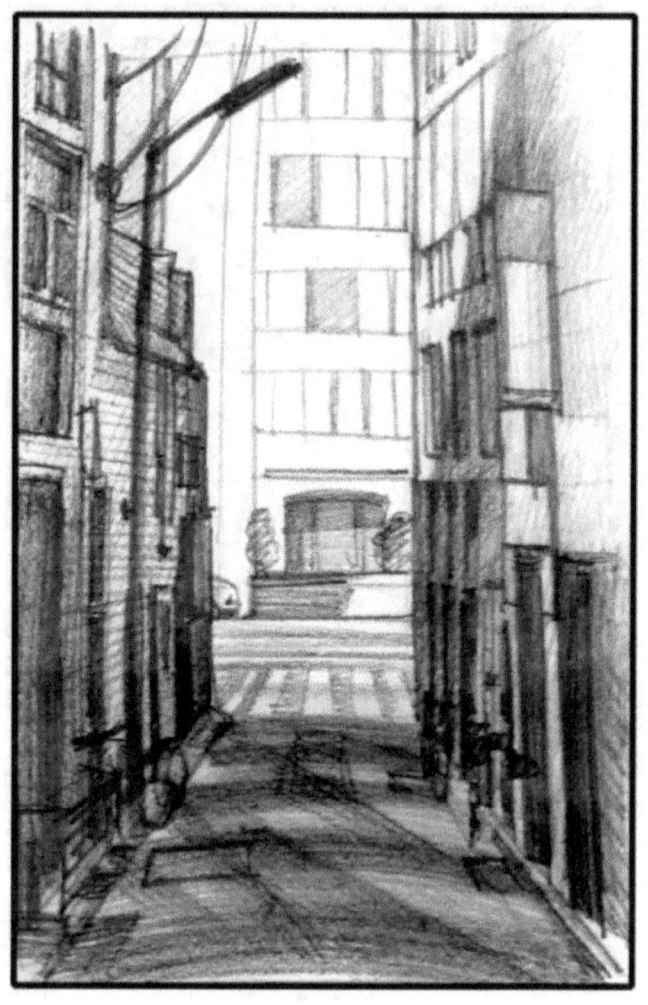

For these landscapes you will need ultimate patience and attention to detail but most of all just experiment and have fun with it.

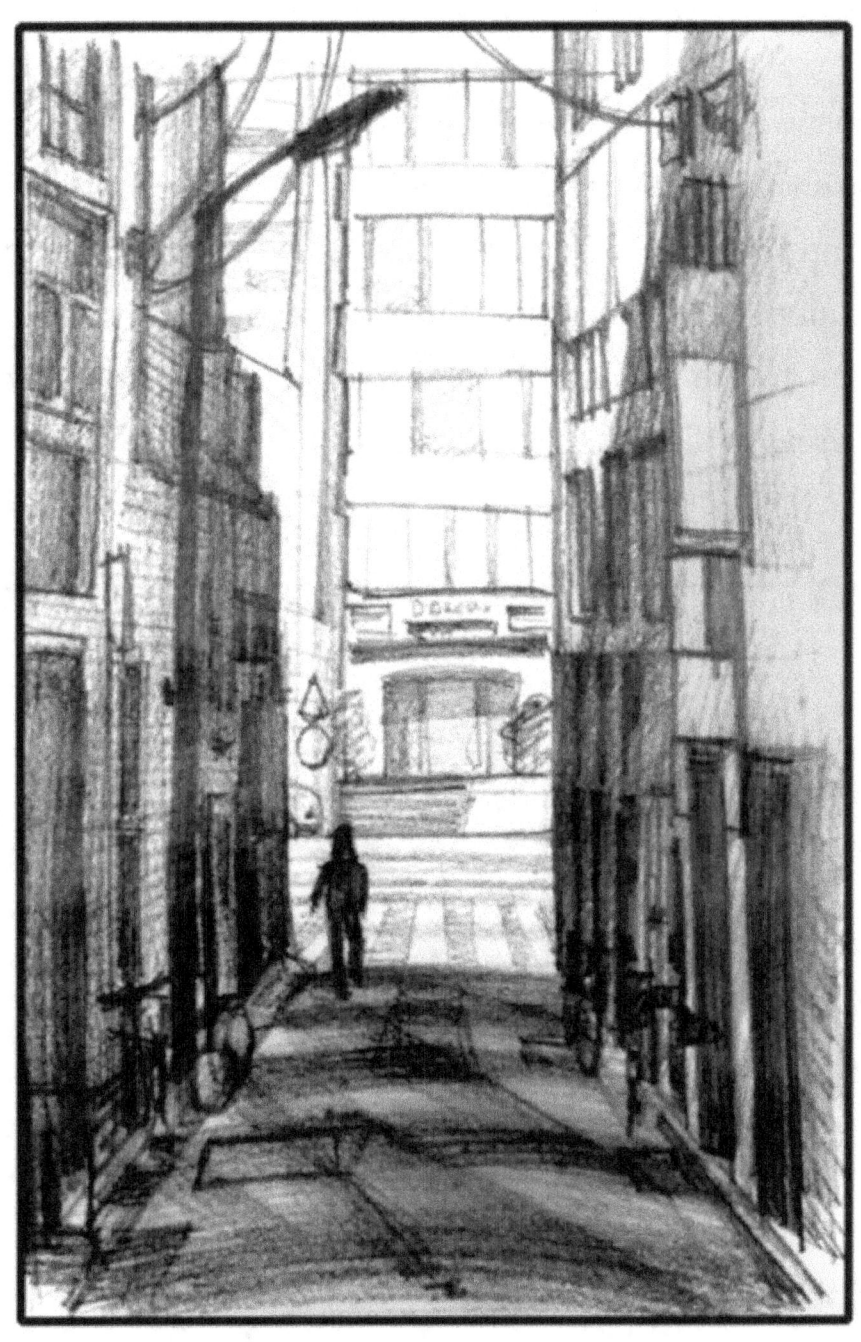

Picture 35. Mountain Ridge

This image is slightly easier in scope than the last, but it is also a very beautiful landscape. You will start out with the outline of the mountain ridge, and then start shading in the distant background. Remember that this is a section of work that you will want to use blending on rather religiously. Especially there are on areas of distant backgrounds.

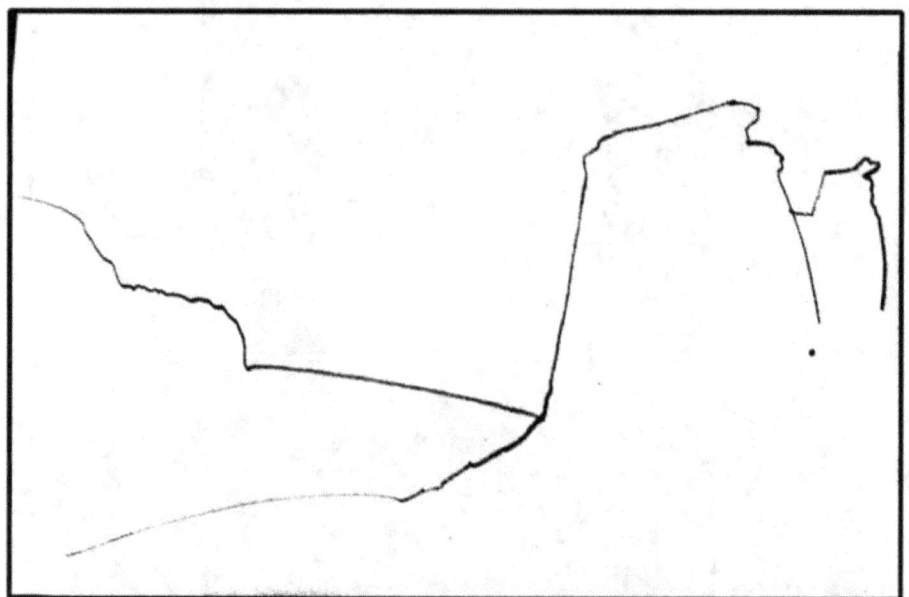

Once you've done that it's time to start adding in the features of the close background such as shrubbery and rocks, as well as the texture of the dirt roads and sand as you would see on the ground and on the rock faces (a, b).

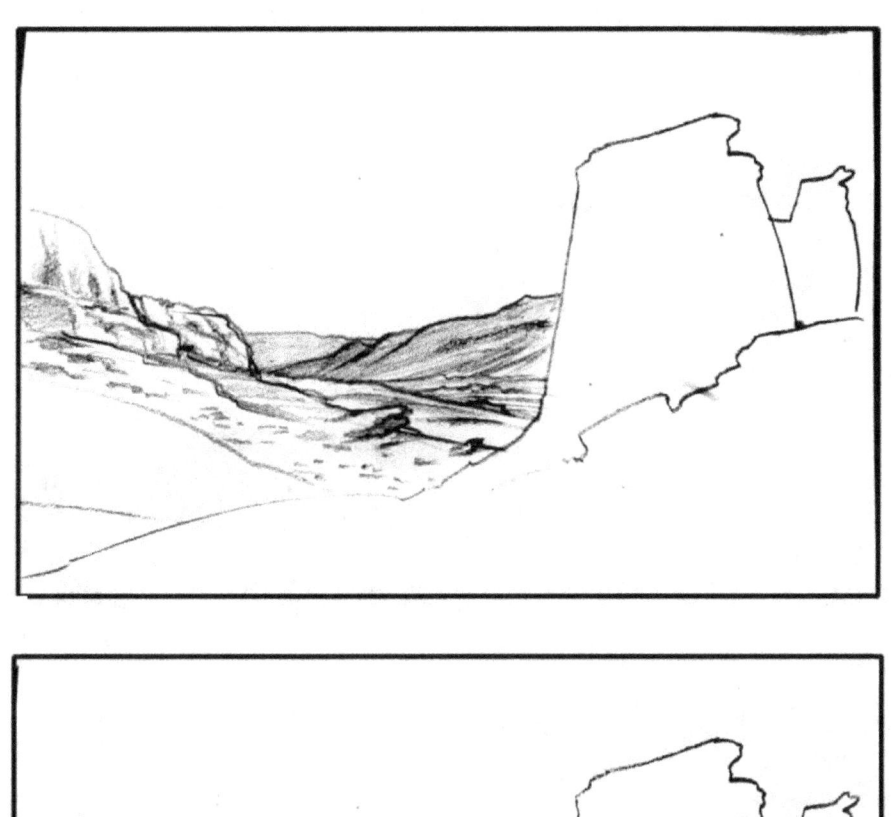

a)

b)

The fourth step is important because it sees you adding the first bit of detail to the actual rock face; here you see some darker shading added in as well as some serious texturizing to the image. This is important when doing nature landscapes because you want it to look like somewhere you could actually go.

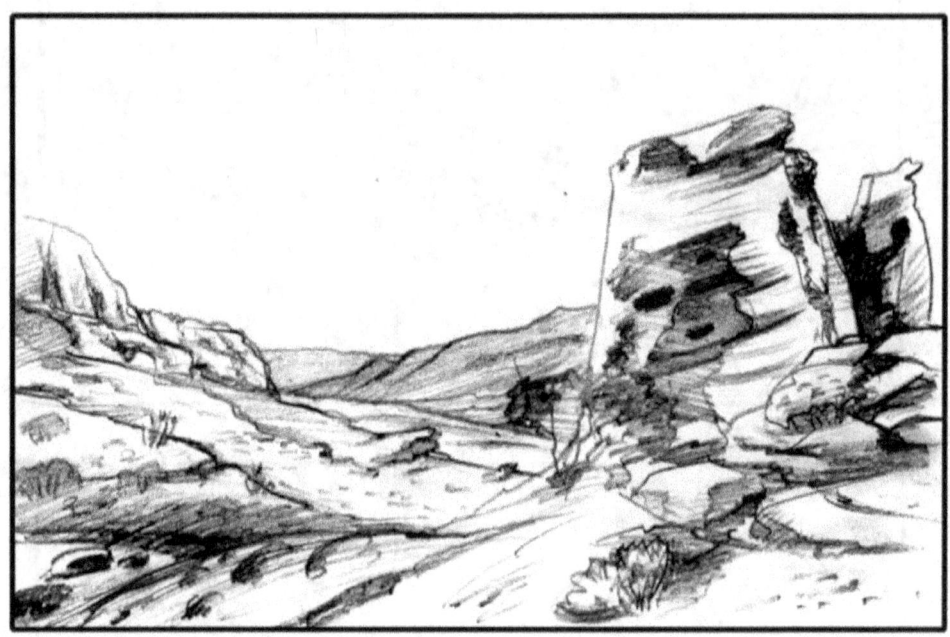

This last step is entirely about the sky, this is a nice looking sky, with some light shading at the top with the gradients lightening up as it goes down to the actual earth. This is another area where you will want to use a lot of subtle but strong blending.

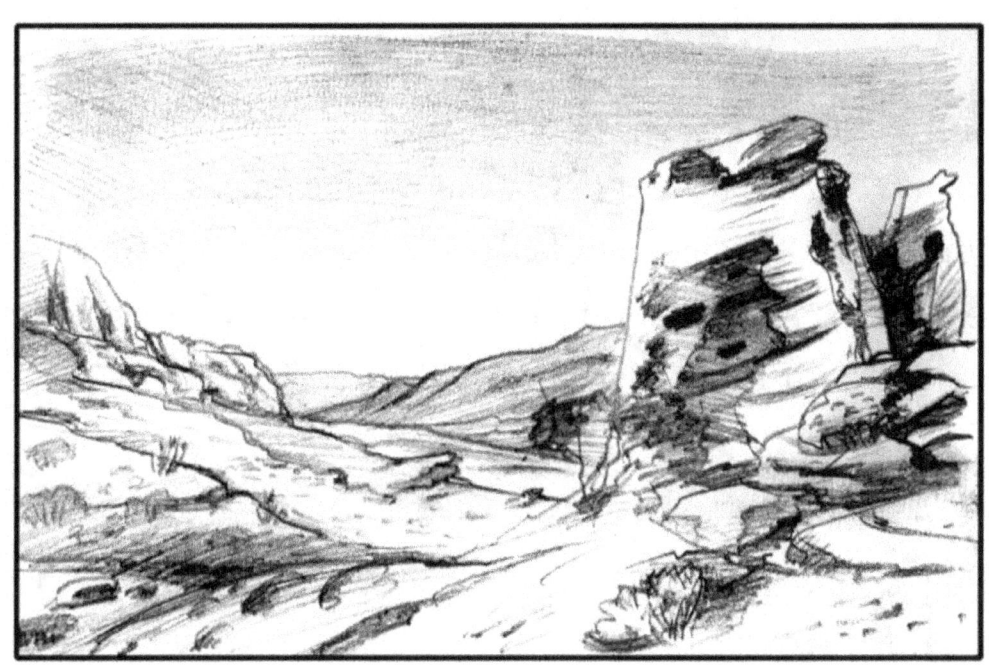

Picture 36. Valley Road

This is a rather nice and interesting looking landscape to add into the mix. This one doesn't rely on any outlines and is almost made entirely from shading and detailing. To make my point look at the very first step, it's a penciled in background with the ridge of trees and bushes shaded in and everything.

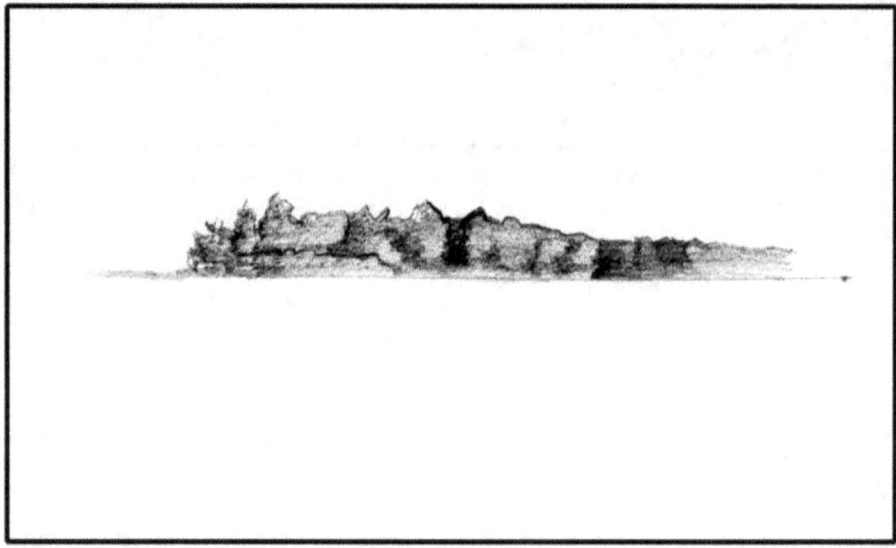

The next step after that is to lightly outline the road but also to shade in the trees on either side of that initial ridge that we drew in to start out.

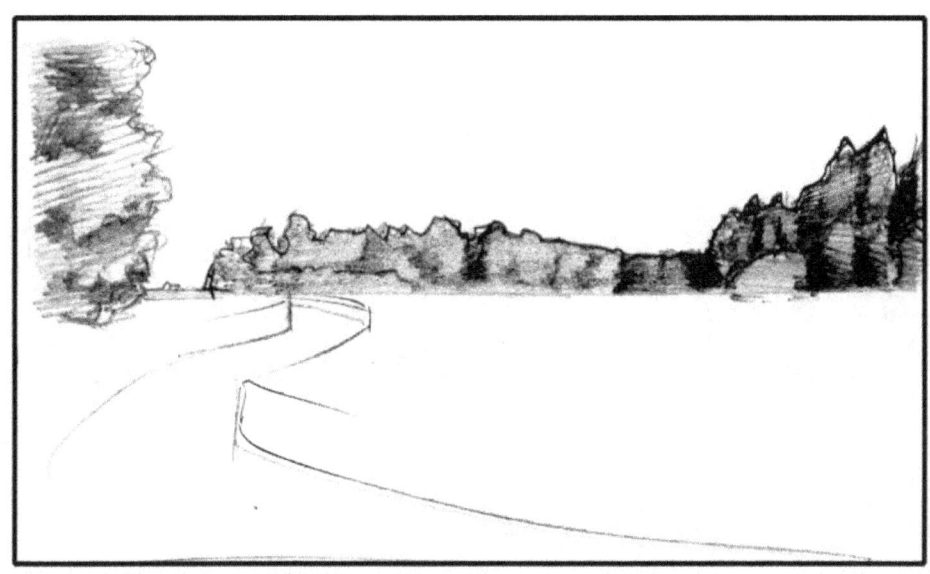

The third step is to actually draw in all the detail of that valley road; the texturizing is very thick here with lots of rocks and foliage surrounding the trail as well (a). You've got divots in the dirt and track marks all over the trail which require their own independent shading and texturing (b).

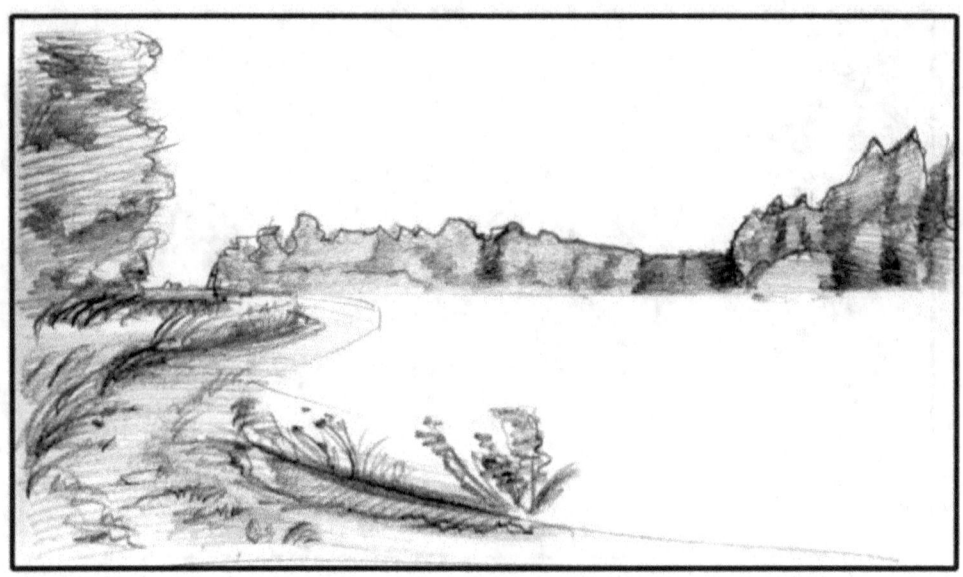

a)

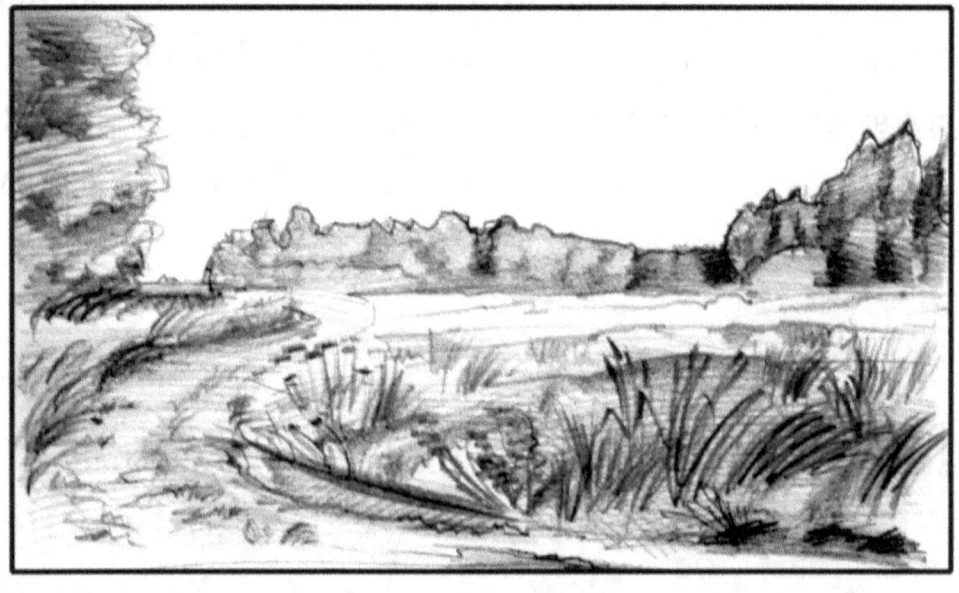

b)

The final step is to really beef up the shading on all the foliage and add the sky in. This sky is a very cloudy looking sky. The clouds are also shaded in very well here too, with proper texturing on them to make them look very full and distant.

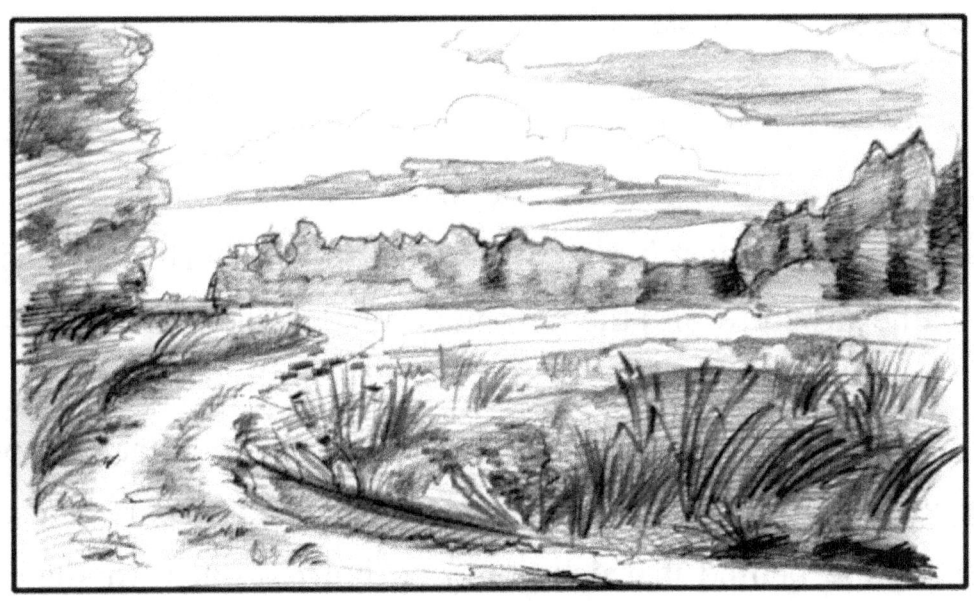

The thing to take away from the landscape is mostly the detail and the heavy shading, this image has you spending most of the time with the pencil shading then it does actually drawing, but that's alright because a lot of the detail required revolves around setting the tone of the landscape.

Picture 37. Ruin Structure

This is the last and final image in this workbook and also my personal favorite landscape. Not just because it's the last one but because it's the most interesting one of them all. This starts out as a lone structure, and them we build up the woods around it.

Start with the structure brick by brick. You can see that each one is individually shaded in and structured that way. There is also a background behind it which is mostly blurred out with shading but is there to add texture.

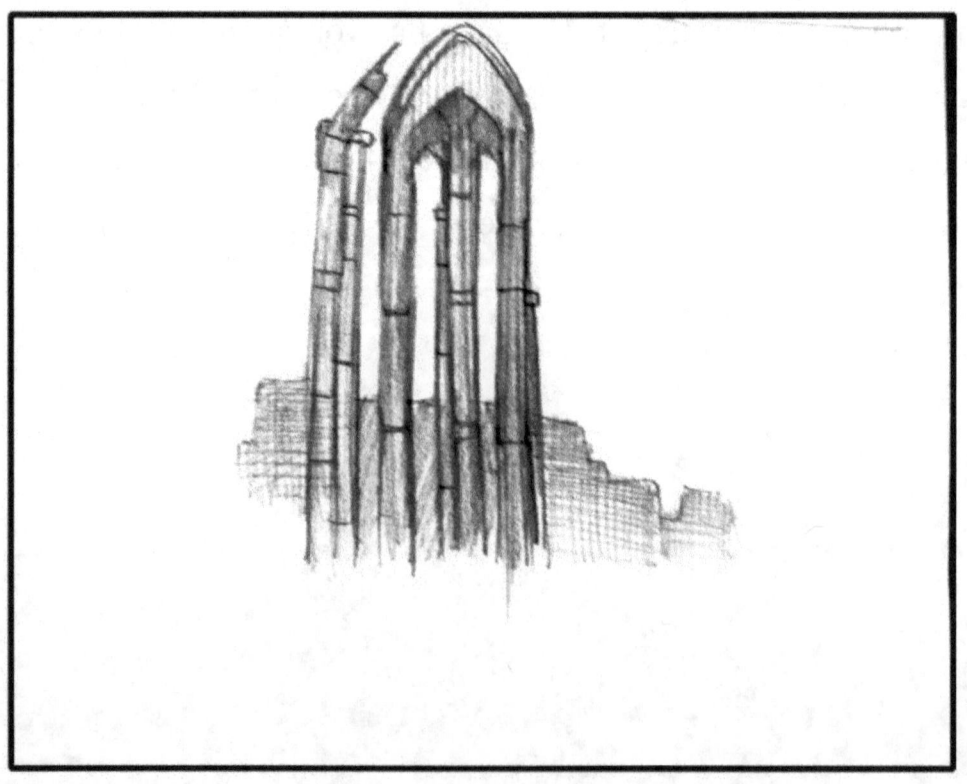

Next we shade in the space behind the structure, keeping it darkest near the ground and lightening up as it spreads out, then we get to add our first sets of outlines.

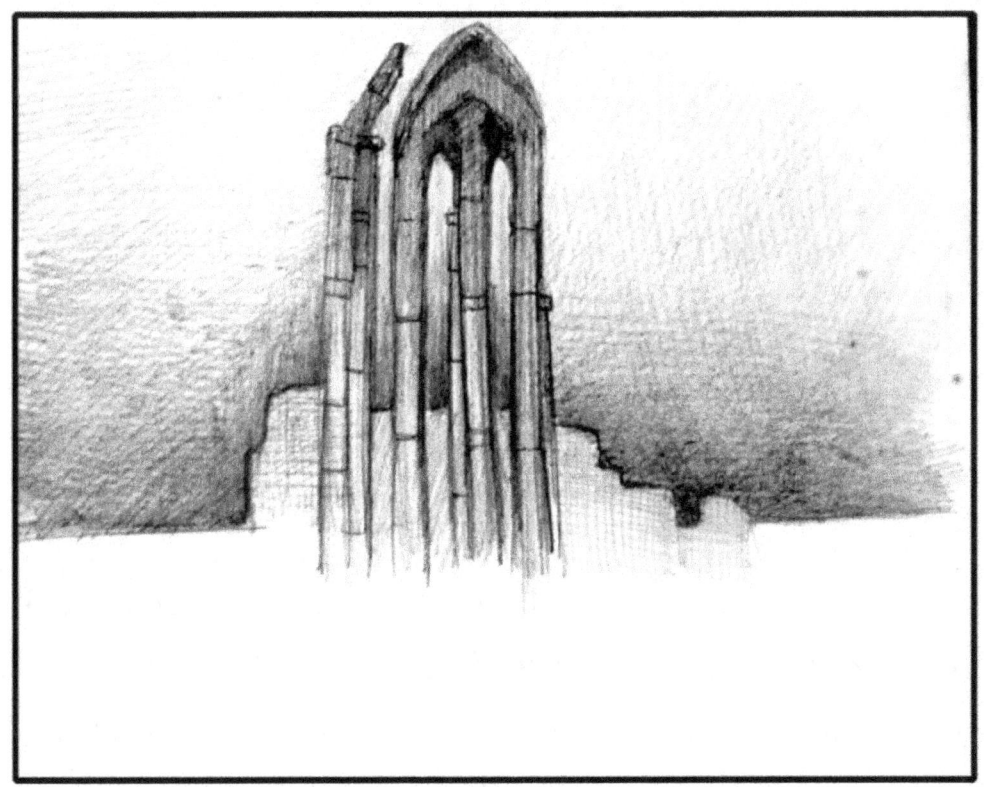

These outlines are impressive because they are just simple trees without leaves, dead trees. Once the outlines are done you start shading them in, making them almost black but saving that for the trees closest to the front of the image.

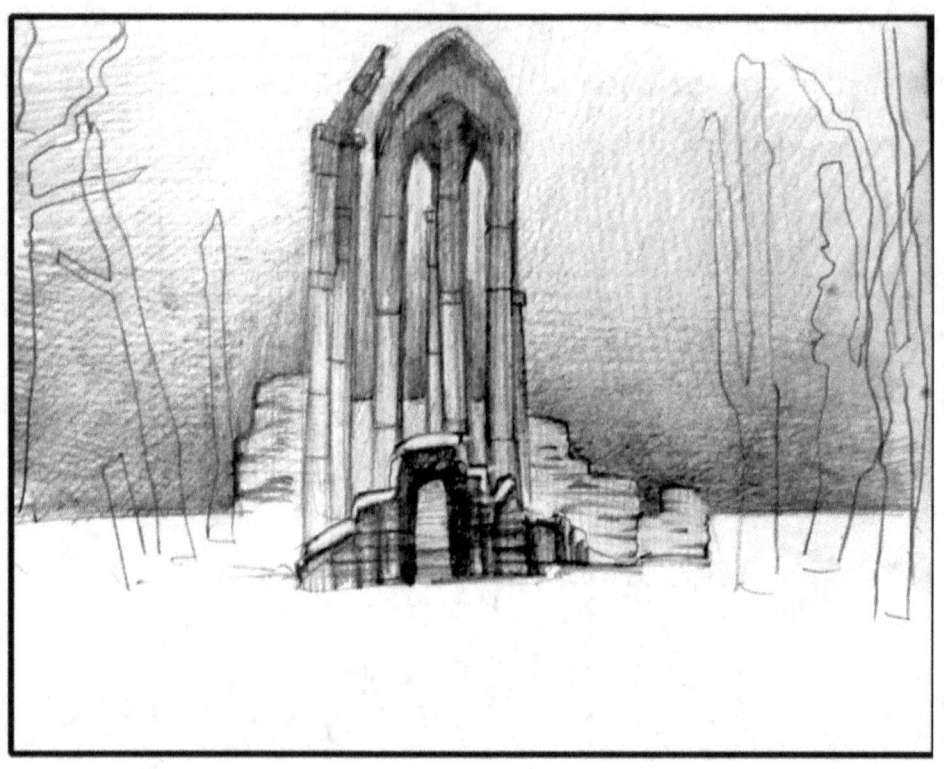

You can even see what looks like a tombstone added into the final step on the right hand side. The big trees added right in the front of the image are the most interesting addition because the interrupt the view of the structure but the mostly make the landscape that much more interesting.

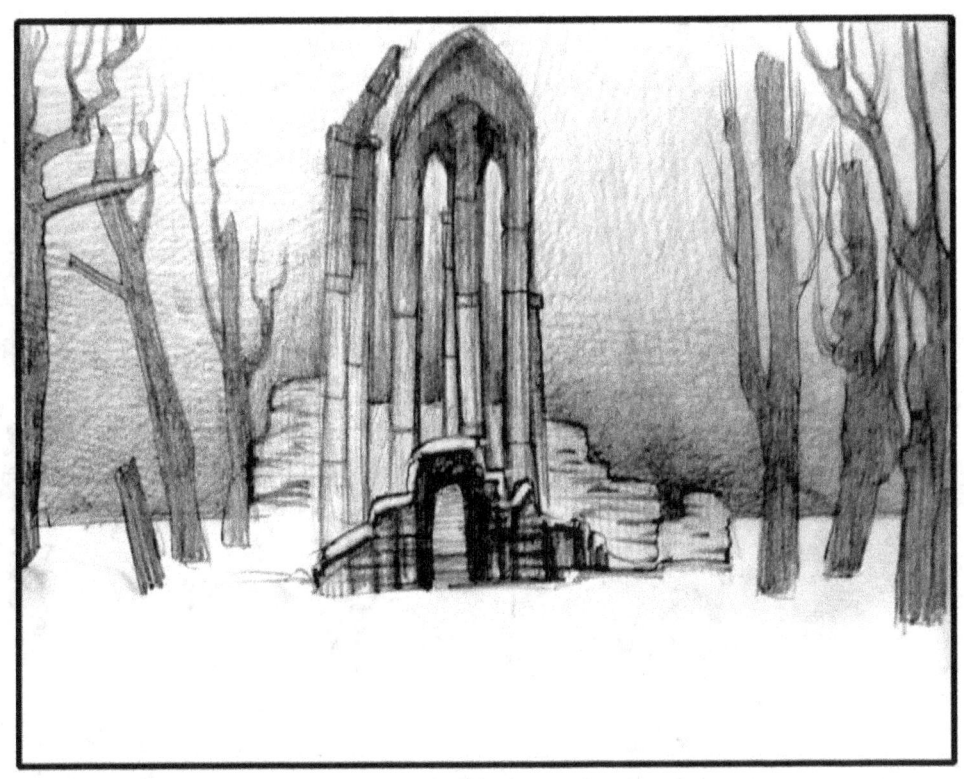

Excellent work on this image and in this section, these aren't the easiest landscapes but they are the most interesting ones to work on and to keep trying your hand at to see how you improve.

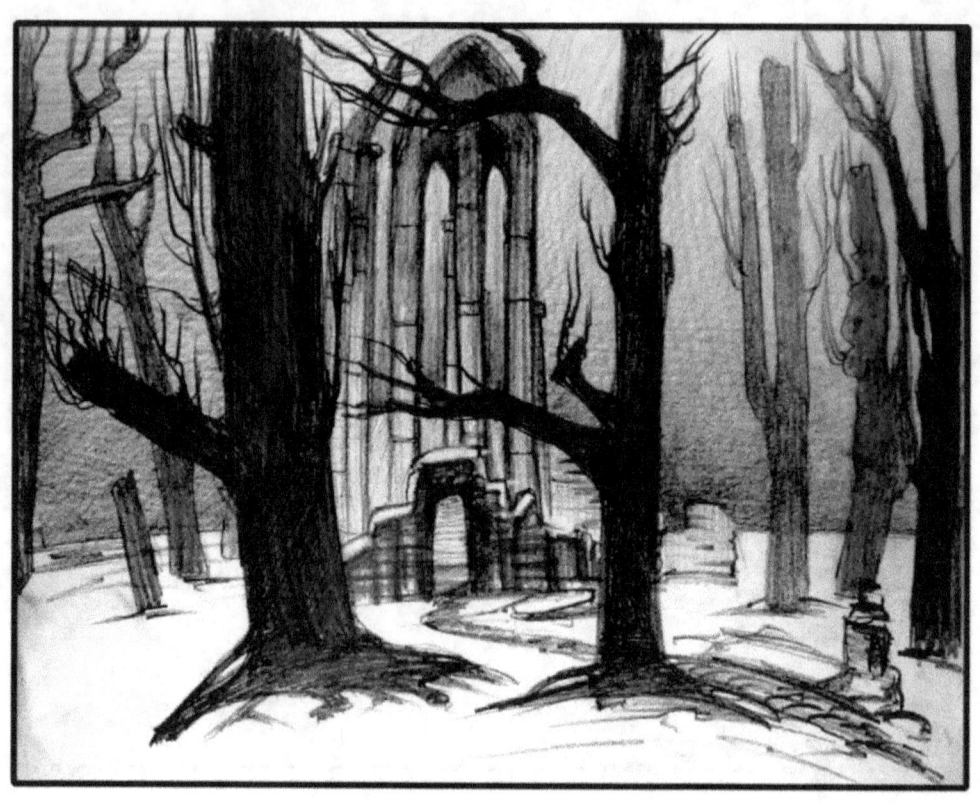

Conclusion

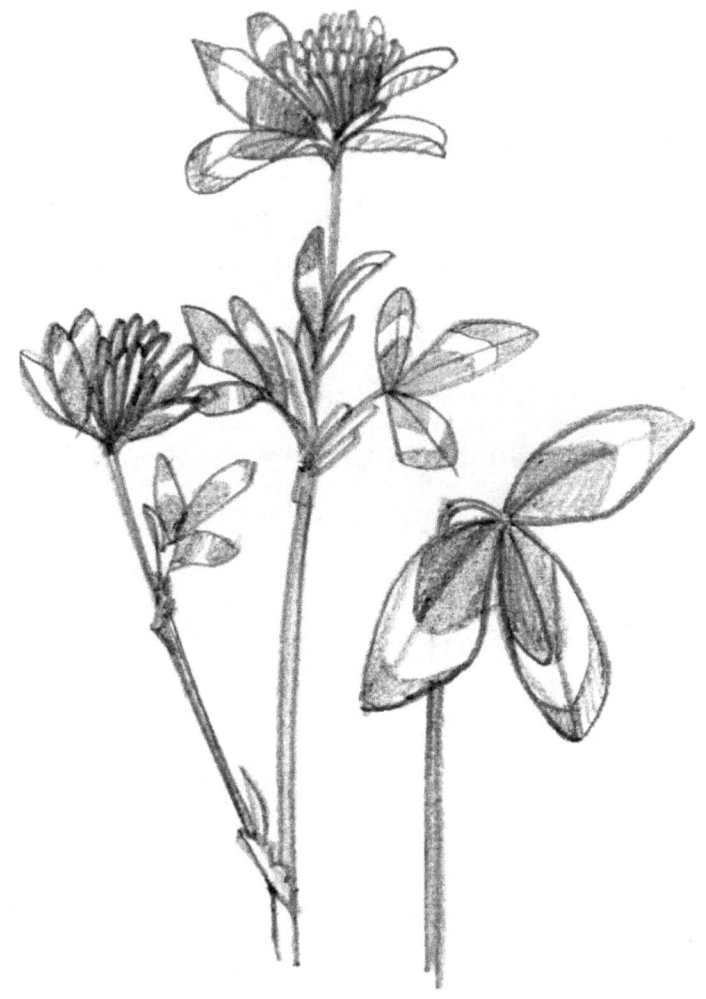

That wraps up the drawing sections of this book! You did it; you drew every single drawing within these pages and learned all of the tips and tricks and techniques of how to master beginning drawing of Nature. You can draw pictures from animals, flowers and trees to the beautiful landscapes. These are drawings that will never go out of style, you can always turn back to these pages to hone your skill and sharpen your tools if you ever spend too much time away from art. However, if you've made it to this final page then my belief is that the draw of art is too strong of a pull for you and you'll be spending a lot more time working on these images and then images of your own that you find out in the world around you! Keep drawing and pursuing the artistic ventures around you in the world, and remember the skills you learned in these pages, from the techniques to the terminology to the utilization of the skills, it will serve you in almost all medium of artistic expression and its invaluable knowledge in reference to drawing. Now get out there and draw the world!

Thank you!

Thank you for choosing our book.

If you liked the book, please leave your feedback on **AMAZON.COM**

We would really appreciate this!

If you would like to have a bonus – **FREE BOOK**, please send the screenshot or the link of your review to this e-mail:

gloria.kemer@gmail.com and we will send you a **FREE BOOK** in PDF as a **GIFT!****

If you want to receive coloring book, please mention it in your message.

** in the e-mail subject please mention the name of the book you reviewed and the author.

www.ingramcontent.com/pod-product-compliance
Lightning Source LLC
Chambersburg PA
CBHW062216220526
45471CB00009B/3224